Chasing Perfection

THE PRINCIPLES BEHIND WINNING
FOOTBALL THE DE LA SALLE WAY

BOB LADOUCEUR
WITH NEIL HAYES

TRIUMPH
BOOKS

Library of Congress Cataloging-in-Publication Data

Ladouceur, Bob, 1954–
  Chasing perfection : the leadership principles behind America's most successful football program / Bob Ladouceur, with Neil Hayes.
    pages cm
  ISBN 978-1-62937-166-5
  1. De La Salle High School (Concord, Calif.)—Football. 2. Football—California—Concord. 3. Ladouceur, Bob, 1954– 4. Football—Coaching. 5. Football—Coaching—Philosophy. 6. Success. 7. Leadership. I. Hayes, Neil, 1967– II. Title.
  GV958.D4L33 2015
  796.3309794—dc23
                                        2015019771

This book is available in quantity at special discounts for your group or organization. For further information, contact:

Triumph Books LLC
814 North Franklin Street
Chicago, Illinois 60610
(312) 337-0747
www.triumphbooks.com

Printed in U.S.A.

ISBN: 978-1-62937-166-5

Page production by Patricia Frey

To Lissa, Suzy, Cathy, Tom, Liz, Pat, Greg, Jake, Olivia, and Brooke, and my children— Jennifer, Danny, Michael, and Sophia. I love you all. Thanks for being my inspiration.

Strange is our situation here upon Earth. Each of us comes for a short visit, not knowing why, yet sometimes seeming to a divine purpose. From the standpoint of daily life, however, there is one thing we do know: that we are here for the sake of other men.

—Albert Einstein

Contents

Foreword

I was so interested in De La Salle High School's football program and coach Bob Ladouceur's success that I found a way to get an advance copy of Neil Hayes' book *When the Game Stands Tall: The Story of the De La Salle Spartans and Football's Longest Winning Streak* back in 2003. My entire family read it.

We were so inspired by what we read that my son, Joe, and I decided to make a documentary about the program in order to share Ladouceur's story of success with as many people as possible. The result was *151: The Greatest Streak*, which aired on ESPN in 2004. And then Hollywood producer David Zelon was so impressed with Hayes' book and our documentary that he made it his mission to make *When the Game Stands Tall* into a major motion picture in 2014 starring Jim Caviezel, Michael Chiklis, Laura Dern, and Alexander Ludwig.

In some ways, however, the story still wasn't complete. The book, our documentary, and the movie focused on the important life lessons such as commitment, dedication, responsibility, and brotherhood that serve as the foundation of the program. But it wasn't until Ladouceur, with the help of Hayes, put his own words to paper that a more complete picture was revealed.

As everybody knows, football is a game fueled by paranoia. Playbooks are guarded, and gameplans are top secret. That's what makes the pages that follow such a treasure. Ladouceur pulls back the curtain on the game's greatest dynasty, revealing everything he learned during a 33-year head-coaching career that produced an astounding 399–25–3 career record.

In this book Ladouceur not only outlines everything from hiring a staff to his philosophies on discipline, motivation, leadership, player development, offense, defense, and special teams, but also explains the specific drills, techniques, and conditioning regimens that have resulted in De La Salle playing the game at what I consider to be the highest level in terms of execution, discipline, and effort.

That's right. I have been a professional coach or broadcaster for more than four decades, but when it comes to the fundamentals of blocking, tackling, and getting off the ball, Ladouceur's teams at De La Salle High School in Concord, California, play on a level that often exceeds college and pro teams. That's why I consider Ladouceur one of the greatest coaches of any sport.

We often think of football as a complicated game. If there's one thing to take from this book, it's that it doesn't have to be. There's nothing complex about how Ladouceur teaches the game. His genius is in his ability to reduce the game to its essence.

This book offers an incredible, time-tested blueprint for aspiring coaches and is a great contribution to the coaching profession. It should be required reading for anybody who wants to coach football—or any sport—for that matter. His valuable lessons about leadership, motivation, commitment, accountability, integrity, hard work, and teamwork will also resonate in the business world.

—John Madden

Introduction

I give Neil Hayes' book, *When the Game Stands Tall: The Story of the De La Salle Spartans and Football's Longest Winning Streak*, a lot of credit for ending our national record 151-game winning streak. Butch Goncharoff, the coach at Bellevue High School in Bellevue, Washington, defeated us in the 2004 season opener by emulating us. He read Hayes' book, and they matched our offseason work ethic, our explosion off the ball, and, most importantly, our commitment to each other, and his team reached a never-before-approached level of performance. Afterward, I couldn't help but think: *Good for them.*

I want everybody to play good football—not just us.

I'm frequently asked how I was able to take over a football program at De La Salle High School in Concord, California, that had never had a winning season and then post a 399–25–3 career record by the time I stepped down 34 years later. I've heard that question even more frequently since *When the Game Stands Tall* became a movie.

I never knew how to respond. Even after all these years, it has remained somewhat of a mystery, even to me. From now on, however, I will refer people to this book because its pages contain everything I learned while compiling the highest winning percentage (.934) in history, winning 19 state championships and five mythical national championships.

I don't believe you can be truly successful if you focus solely on winning. In my opinion, a successful program must be about more than outcomes. Kids will fight for you and will achieve amazing things if you stand for more than that. It's about getting kids to play together, work together toward a common goal, and mature into adults. We were never fighting for wins. We were fighting for a belief in what we stood for, the way we believe life should be lived and people should be treated. Winning is a by-product of how you approach life and relationships.

I've learned that creating a culture of commitment and accountability is the best way to help young men mature into respectful, responsible, productive adults who are better equipped to overcome adversity in their private lives. I can't stress this enough.

The knowledge gained from excelling in this type of environment is burned into the hearts and minds of everyone who fully participates. We measure our success by how well we have embraced the essence of accountability and commitment and the relationships that spawns.

It creates a passion because wherever our players go they know they are connected to a group of people who love, respect, and accept them. I stand on our sideline sometimes in utter amazement as I watch our players push themselves far beyond what they previously thought was possible all because they felt connected to others who care.

My first piece of advice for anybody who teaches, coaches, or manages others in the business world is a lesson I was fortunate to learn early in my career. As a young coach, I thought winning games and championships would give me a greater sense of self-worth, but I was still unfulfilled. My program didn't reach its potential, and I didn't find self-satisfaction until I quit focusing on what I was getting out of it and began focusing on how the kids were benefitting.

I always wanted to make a difference, not only with my own players but on a larger scale, which is why we have always had an open-door policy at De La Salle. If there's something you can take from us that helps you as a coach, or benefits a player or your program, that's a win-win situation to me. But there's one point I want to make clear: we're not telling you how to run your football program. I'm just telling you how *I* operated mine, and how my successor, Justin Alumbaugh, and longtime defensive coordinator and special teams coach Terry Eidson, continue to do it today.

The release of the book *When the Game Stands Tall* brought a lot of attention to our program, and the movie by the same name brought more. We already field hundreds of emails every year asking how we motivate players, how we run our offseason conditioning program, and how our offensive line gets off the line so quickly. I've done my best to explain it all here.

I can honestly say that while looking back on my career I have no regrets. If I had to do it all over again, I would do it exactly the same way I did it and the way I've outlined it here.

—Bob Ladouceur

(Photo by Bob Larson)

De La Salle Coaching Staff

Bob Ladouceur—*former head coach*
In 33 years at De La Salle High School, Ladouceur established himself as one of the most successful high school coaches in the country. His 399–25–3 record includes the most victories in California history, 29 North Coast Section Championships, and 19 California State Championships. His team's 151-game winning streak between 1992 and 2004 is the longest in the history of high school sports. Both *USA TODAY* and FOX Sports voted De La Salle the No. 1 team in the nation on five different occasions with the Spartans finishing in the top 20 every year for the last 21 years of his head coaching career. Ladouceur was inducted into the National Federation of State High School Associations' Hall of Fame in 2001. Ladouceur has been a full-time instructor of religious studies and physical education at De La Salle. In 1998 he was awarded the Warren Ukel Educator of the Year Award for Contra Costa County. He has a bachelor's degree from San Jose State, a master's degree from Saint Mary's (California) College, and an honorary doctorate from San Jose State.

Justin Alumbaugh—*head coach*
Alumbaugh assumed the head coaching position when Bob Ladouceur stepped down after the 2012 season. He began his coaching career shortly after his graduation from De La Salle, where he was a three-year starter and captain of the 1997 team that broke the national record of 73 consecutive victories. Alumbaugh has a bachelor's degree in history from UCLA and a master's in history from San Francisco State. He teaches English and social studies.

Joe Aliotti—*quality control coach*
Aliotti has coached at Boise State, Oregon State, and Pittsburg (California) High School and has been an assistant at De La Salle since 1998. Aliotti, who also serves as De La Salle's dean of students, quarterbacked Boise State to the Division I-AA national championship in 1980.

Doug Bauman—*assistant athletic trainer*
A Sonoma State University and University of North Carolina-Greensboro graduate, Bauman started working at De La Salle in 2008. He is also a member of the school's faculty, teaching courses in beginning sports medicine, advance sports medicine, sports medicine 3, and health/first aid.

Donnie Boyce—*secondary and special teams/kicking coach*
Boyce has been a De La Salle assistant coach since 2004. Before that he was an assistant at Rio Vista (California) High School for five years.

Chris Crespi—*scouting coordinator and scout team coach*
Crespi played linebacker and guard during Ladouceur's first two seasons at De La Salle. He returned to his alma mater in 2013 after a 10-year career as a Wall Street research analyst. The former University of California-Davis captain and honorable mention All-American earned an MBA from Northwestern University and is a substitute teacher at De La Salle.

Tony DeMattei—*video coordinator*
DeMattei, who works as a CPA and is a partner in a real estate company, has a passion for film and video. He began videotaping games while his son was playing at De La Salle and was later asked to assist in the program's transition from analog to digital video. He has been taping De La Salle practices and games since 2010.

Terry Eidson—*defensive and special teams coordinator*

Eidson has been an assistant football coach at De La Salle since 1981. He has been the varsity special teams coach since 1982. Since taking over as defensive coordinator in 1992, De La Salle has gone 291–12–2. His defenses have allowed an average of 11 points per game during that time while recording 74 shutouts. A religious studies teacher, Eidson received a bachelor's degree in political science from UCLA and a master's in theology at Saint Mary's College.

Steve Jacoby—*defensive line coach*

A former Saint Mary's College player, assistant coach, and associate athletic director, Jacoby has been at De La Salle since 2007. Before that he was at Skyline High School in Oakland, California, for three seasons.

Kent Mercer—*head athletic trainer*

Mercer was an assistant athletic trainer at De La Salle from 1998 through 2001 and has been head athletic trainer since 2001. He also has served as director of rehabilitation of the Muir Orthopedic Specialists since 2001.

Mark Panella—*quarterbacks coach*

Panella was the quarterback on Ladouceur's 1984 team and has been quarterbacks coach since 1993. He designed the numbering system for the passing game. The De La Salle Hall of Fame member graduated from the University of Denver where he pitched on the varsity baseball team.

Dr. Charles Preston—*team physician*

Dr. Preston completed his orthopedic training at NYU Hospital for Joint Diseases after earning both his undergraduate and medical degrees at University of California-Irvine. While in New York, Dr. Preston was the house physician at Shea Stadium for the Mets and Madison Square Garden. He is the founding medical director of the Sports Performance Institute at San Ramon Regional Medical Center.

Blake Tuffli—*mental skills and receivers coach*
Tuffli has been coaching receivers at De La Salle since 2006. Before that, he was an assistant coach at California High School and at Diablo Valley College. Tuffli has a master's degree in sports psychology.

Mark Wine—*strength training and conditioning coach*
Wine has been the head strength and conditioning coach at De La Salle since 2012 while also serving in the same capacity for Team USA Synchronized Swimming, the Walnut Creek Soccer Club, and the Haiti Polo team. The owner of Functional Muscle Fitness in Concord, California, Wine has also worked with the Oakland Raiders and Texas Longhorns football teams.

CHAPTER 1

Laying the Foundation

The game of football is about defeating the man in front of you. Everything else plays out from there.

—Former De La Salle head coach Bob Ladouceur

I believe football is in my DNA. I understood the game from the get-go, even as a small child. I can remember back to my days growing up in suburban Detroit, Michigan, wearing a plastic Lions helmet and shoulder pads and running around the front lawn playing football. I loved it. I never lost that passion for it. In a lot of ways, I felt I was meant to do this.

I have tried to figure out why that was true for me. There were two subjects in high school that I really excelled at. One was physics, and one was geometry. The game is about physics and geometry, and I truly believe that helped and aided me throughout all those years. The only math class I ever excelled in in high school was geometry. It was easy for me. In every other mass class, I struggled. Geometry was the only science class I excelled in was physics. I just understood leverage, how to move mass, and things like that. I really think there's a strong connection between those two subjects and the game of football.

I have always been able to see where defenses are vulnerable and how you can layer a defense. I've always understood the angles and steps required to properly execute a trap block, when a quarterback should throw and at what angle, and the physics and body position involved to move a guy bigger than you.

Know the Game

I was fortunate to have great high school coaches in Fred Houston and Pete Villa. I had great college coaches in Daryll Rogers and Dick Mannini. These guys taught the game well. I understood the game. I understood how the pieces fit together. I wasn't a great player in college. I was a good player in high school and in college I was a role guy. I played special teams. I played offense until I had two knee surgeries, and then they switched me to defense. I was willing to make the transition. I backed up guys and I learned. So at 24 when they put me in charge of this program, I thought, *I know this game. I can teach these kids something.*

That's what carried me when I started. I had a good working knowledge of the game and I could tell what was working, what wasn't, why our defensive line was playing poorly, why our offensive line was blocking so well, why our receivers could or could not run a good route. I understood it all. I had no experience, but that first year in 1979, those kids looked at me and said, "This guy knows something about this game." They felt like I could teach them something and they liked that. They trusted me and gave me the benefit of the doubt as I fumbled through my early years.

Because I was a running back before being a defensive back at San Jose State, I knew the running back and quarterback positions. I knew all the defensive back positions and I knew some stuff about linebackers. I was less sure about the offensive and defensive lines, the receivers, and special teams, but as I went on, I schooled myself until I felt like I could coach every position on the field.

We had a great offensive line coach in Steve Alexakos, and the technique we currently use was his idea. He left in 1992 to coach at San Jose State. I loved what he was doing, so before I took over his spot as offensive line coach, I worked with him for two weeks. I knew a lot about what he was doing after working with him for three years and calling the offense and watching his guys work, but I wanted to know the minutiae and the methodology of what he was teaching. He was a good teacher. He taught me everything, and for the next 10 years, I personally coached the offensive line. I felt really shaky going into it that first year, but I got used to it, and that stretch of coaching was the most rewarding and most fun I ever had. A head coach should be able to step in for any position coach, and that group should not miss a beat.

There's an adage that Alexakos used: you have to inspect what you expect. You have to know when things are breaking down and why they're breaking down if you're a head coach. You have to know it all down to the minute details. A good coach has to know exactly what he's looking for and what his expectations are. There's a lot kids don't know, but they do know whether you know the game. You can't fake it. You can't fool them. They will respect you and listen to you if you know what you're talking about and they appreciate it most when you work with them to correct their bad habits and reinforce their positive ones. They think, *This guy wants me to be a better player and he's working with me to do it. I'll give him the effort.*

The Game Remains the Same

If there's one thing I've learned, it's that the game is always the same. It will never change. No matter what offense you're running, it's always going to boil down to old-school building blocks. *Can you block? Can you tackle? Can you run? Can you get off blocks? Can you get your guys in the right spots?*

That's exactly what we work on. We pour all our energy into technique and developing our players. We teach our kids how to get off blocks every day in practice. I tell my linebackers, "I never want to hear you say you got blocked. They are going to send guys to block you. The key is to defeat that block and make the hit. You're an inside linebacker. That's your *job*. Defeat the block and make the tackle."

We teach them how to do that. There's a technique to it. We drill it every day. Strike, get off your block, fill your gap. If the ball goes the other way, cross his face, gap exchange back the other way. Whatever you do, don't run around the block. Then we watch film on Saturday and say, "Your head was on the wrong side when that guy was blocking you. Now you're cut off. You just wrecked the integrity of the defense. Now that tackle has a free release into our linebacker" or "This is why you got cut off, you knucklehead, you stepped with the wrong foot." Those are the things we concentrate on. Those are the things we're constantly correcting. The stuff we do is simple. Nothing we do is complex. We're high school football coaches, but our emphasis is on technique.

Everybody wants to be a success. I've never heard anyone say he or she wants to be a failure. No matter what their definition of success might be—and it's different for everybody—everybody wants to be successful. People often ask me the secret to my success. I'm always baffled by that because there is no secret. I tell that to our players: "We're going to go out and play this big game tomorrow night. We can't sprinkle you with fairy dust. This is going to be your gig. You have to earn it and work for it."

For us, for me, our foundation for success is grueling, nose-to-the-grindstone, monotonous, tedious work and trying to get

We drills our kids ad nauseam to make sure they assume the correct three-point stance. (Photo by Bob Larson)

the fundamentals and the foundation right. It requires a ton of conditioning, weight training, and preparation. And once you get into practice, it's drilling and re-drilling ad nauseam to the point of boredom. I feel brain-dead after practices. There's no way around that. No matter what your system is, there has to be a foundation of technique and fundamentals. That's what the game requires. There's no way to get that unless you drill, and that's hard, physically and mentally exhausting work.

It's Not About You

I had 399 wins when I stepped down as head coach. Everybody wanted to know why I didn't stick around for a milestone 400th win. The truth is, I never considered it. What difference would one more win make? I guess that number has a strange significance to some, but to me, it was fitting because coaching was never about wins or numbers. I didn't announce my plans to step down until after the season because I didn't want my last year to become some cheesy motivational ploy for the players or to draw media attention.

Coaches often preach the importance of teamwork, selflessness, humility, sincerity, and accountability, but it starts with them. If a coach doesn't exemplify those traits, his players never will.

How much do you care about people? What are we here for?

People ask me all the time why I didn't go on to coach in college or the pros. I never got rich working at De La Salle, that's for sure, but I never tried to be a college or pro coach because that's not why I got into it. I always wanted to work with kids. There's a special innocence to kids and a thirst to become somebody—even if they're not sure what. Our former players who have gone on to play in college or in the NFL always come back and say the same thing: "It's not the same. This is where I had the most fun. This is where it all meant the most."

That's because the high school years are a special period in a person's life. Young adults make dramatic changes between the ages of 14 and 18 both physically and emotionally, and they need good people around them to work with them and guide them, good people to listen and nudge them in the right direction.

I wanted to use football as a way of making a difference, a way of helping kids grow up so when they graduate from De La Salle they can step into a job as a fully functioning member of a dynamic community. That's what I thought my job was and still do—to prepare these guys so they can go out in the world and raise families, be successful, be happy. The bottom line for a healthy team or a healthy company is a question: how much do you really care about other people? How much do they matter? That's important.

Hiring a Staff

One of the best things I ever learned as a leader is to hire talented coaches who knew what they were doing. It sounds obvious, but you need to hire people who are strong where you are weak. My longtime assistant, Terry Eidson, is an extrovert. I'm an introvert. Our personalities are totally different, but our values and the way we approach the game are identical. That's why we were such a great tandem for 32 years. We disagree on a lot of things but not on the important things.

I never micromanaged my coaches or stood over them and told them what they have to do. I found out if they could do it or not by observing them, listening to them, and watching them with kids. If they could do it, I got out of their way and didn't bother them. I helped mentor people, but once they started to work, I left them alone. I just never did their jobs for them. That's emasculating. I wasn't always 100 percent sure what Terry was doing half the time because I trusted him implicitly and knew he was going to do a great job.

I liked to solicit input from my entire staff. Whenever I made a decision, especially concerning a kid, I always asked everybody's opinion. I always felt six heads were better than one. Somebody might have a better idea than I. A lot of times they did, and I'd go with their recommendation. Then we'd vote on it. Ninety percent of the time it turned out how I wanted it to turn out, but everyone had a say; everyone was invested. I want everyone to believe this is our team and not just my team.

It's also my personality type. I always preferred to make decisions as a group and call it a group decision. It's just smart. Being in a management or leadership position, you want to get people's thoughts and ideas and include them in the process. Otherwise, morale goes through the floor.

Create a Mission Statement

This step is important because it's a great guide for a coach, and it reminds you that you're an educator first and that there's an overall philosophy that's bigger than your program or the game that you must adhere to. Everything you do should emanate from your mission statement.

I adopted the mission statements for both the school as a whole and the athletic department because they aligned seamlessly with my values. I didn't want my mission statement to be separate from the school because I think of football as an extracurricular activity with the ultimate goal being to teach kids something other than just the skills of the game. I always wanted to aim higher than that. Your mission statement boils down to what you believe in as an educator and a person.

Are you about winning football games or about finding teachable moments, maintaining perspective, and shaping character? Here's what I came up with:

DE LA SALLE ATHLETIC DEPARTMENT
MISSION STATEMENT

The athletic department, guided by traditions of the Brothers of the Christian Schools and the charism of Saint John Baptist de La Salle, founder of the Brothers and Patron of Teachers, is committed to providing a well-rounded program that is not only physically challenging but one that further promotes the spiritual academic values of Saint John Baptist de La Salle.

The athletic department recognizes and fosters the development of commitment, brotherhood, sportsmanship, instills in all student-athletes a sense of pride and achievement, and seeks to create an environment in which all student-athletes develop a sense of self-esteem and dignity in a Christian setting that is both moral and caring.

DE LA SALLE HIGH SCHOOL
MISSION STATEMENT

De La Salle High School is a Roman Catholic educational community where students are loved, instructed, and guided according to the traditions of the Brothers of the Christian Schools and the charism of Saint John Baptist de La Salle, founder of the Brothers and Patron of Teachers.

De La Salle High School provides a Catholic, Lasallian education rooted in liberal arts tradition, which prepares young people for life and college. The school seeks to educate students spiritually, academically, physically, and socially through the promotion of a vital faith life, sponsorship of strong academic programs, a wide range of student activities, and the witness of a concerned and dedicated faculty, administration and staff.

De La Salle High School recognizes and promotes the dignity of each student by providing an environment that is moral, caring, and joyful. Within such a setting, the school seeks to challenge its students and serve others, especially the poor, and to deepen a sense of responsibility for humanity's future.

De La Salle High School seeks to serve and embrace students with varied academic needs and diverse social, cultural, and economic backgrounds and does so in partnership with families and all those who are committed to living the Lasallian heritage.

» THE HANDBOOK

I had already been coaching for a decade when I began compiling a coaches' handbook out of necessity. I started to see things happening that I didn't want happening, like coaches coming to practice in ratty jeans or flip-flops. That wasn't how I wanted to approach coaching. Kids are aware of everything. First impressions are important. I wanted to make it clear that the expectations for coaches were the same as for a teacher in a classroom. It just so happens our classroom is a football field.

The handbook I created pertains to coaches on all levels. It is literally our Bible and what we go by. We don't have it at practice in our back pockets and we don't look at it all the time because we know it by heart. This is how we operate.

I. PHILOSOPHY

It is the responsibility of De La Salle football coaches to:

1. Know and adhere to the school's mission statement, philosophy, and school rules.
2. Be an educator first.
3. Promote an education-first philosophy and guide players to become responsible students.
4. Be examples and role models to players and the community.
5. Teach students how to be responsible members of an athletic team.
6. Teach students to play the game of football.
7. Strive to make the game of football fun.

II. PROFESSIONAL RESPONSIBILITIES

1. To dress like a professional
   a. Practice attire—shorts, sweats, tee, or collared shirt. All clothing should be clean and with no holes or rips. School colors are preferred.
   b. Gameday—slacks (no jeans), shirts with collars, school hats.
   c. Clean shaven or hair and beards trimmed.
   d. No tobacco use around students on or off the field.
   e. No drinking or gambling around students on or off the field.

III. COACH-PLAYER RELATIONSHIPS

It is the responsibility of De La Salle football coaches to:

1. Never swear or rage at a player.

2. Know the team rules and goals and enforce the rules consistently and uniformly.
3. Adhere to your own team rules (i.e. being on time.
4. Know players off the field. Be informed about academic life and be informed about home life as much as possible.
5. Never play an injured player. Be able to recognize injuries and administer first aid. Clear all injured or potentially concussed players through a trainer before returning them to the game.
6. Never punish players with physical conditioning.
7. Never physically handle, push, shove, or grab a player.
8. Discipline to be administered as follows:
   - A player will not practice.
   - A player will not start a game.
   - A player will not play in a game.
   - A player will not suit up for a game.
   - A player will turn in his gear.

IV. PRACTICE GUIDELINES
It is the responsibility of De La Salle coaches to:
1. Be on time to all football functions.
2. Have a weekly and daily practice schedule.
3. Know your coaching responsibilities, including the terminology and techniques of your players.
4. Run drills that are position-specific, have training aids ready and available, know what you're looking for during drills, and correct and/or praise good work.
5. Coach *your* players. Do not coach or comment on players who are not your responsibility except when permission is granted or a player is in danger.

6. Work toward understanding the entire scheme of the offense or defense.
7. Drill technique and fundamentals for the entire season.
8. Not argue with other coaches on the field.
9. Work with the varsity coach who is coaching your area of responsibility if you are a freshman or junior varsity coach.
10. Scout opponents and know their strengths and weaknesses and devise gameplans accordingly.

V. GAMEDAY GUIDELINES
It is the responsibility of De La Salle football coaches to:
1. Be calm. If a coach is excited or out of control, players will not trust or listen to him.
2. Help players during the game by displaying confidence in them. A coach shouldn't be another opponent.
3. Be aware if a player is distracted and his head is not in the game. If a player is distracted, do not yell, pull him from the game.
4. Not yell at officials because it displays poor sportsmanship and therefore makes you a poor role model.
5. Be sure there is a clear plan for substitutions and only place players in positions where they have practice experience.
6. Don't watch the game like a spectator. Watch the players *you* coach.
7. Be aware of player conduct. No cheap shots, trash talk, or taunting—EVER.
8. Not give advice to coordinators in the middle of a series. Have advice procedures worked out before the game.

9. Never speak to a rival coach or opponent during a game.

10. Never allow visitors into the team box.

11. Never run up the score in a mismatch situation.

- In addition to the above, the following pertains to coaches on the JUNIOR VARSITY level:

  1. Players must be aware that weight training is an integral part of De La Salle football, and the weight program must be maintained throughout the entire season.

  2. Team rules must be fair and consistent, and players must be aware of rules and punishments. Rules should include promptness, grades, substance use, classroom, and off-campus behavior.

  3. Players and coaches should address each other with mutual respect. Players should address coaches as "Coach" or "Mister." Coaches should address players by first or last name.

  4. All players should have an offensive and defensive position and should practice at both positions throughout the season.

  5. All coaches should work with varsity coaches to assure that terminology, technique, and drill work is consistent.

  6. Deciding which positions players should play should be discussed with varsity coaches and agreed upon.

  7. Stress to players that they are in a "farm club" system, and their ultimate goal is to start on the varsity someday. Players should be coached and developed with this in mind.

8. Set up time for summer workouts that are conducive for the entire team and not just the coach.
9. Players with "attitude problems" should not start. Players should understand what attitudes are desirable and undesirable. Do not confuse "attitude problem" with a personality conflict with you.
10. Players who are not available for routinely required conditioning should not start. Players must understand conditioning is an important part of the program and mandatory—save extremely special circumstances.
11. Players should know why they are starting or not starting and what they need to do in order to be a starter.
12. Inform parents of team rules, expectations, and injury procedures.

• In addition to the above, the following pertains to coaches at the FRESHMAN level:

1. Inform players that playing football at De La Salle is a privilege and not a right. Teach them about pride and tradition. Pride involves respect for coaches, school facilities, equipment, teachers, J.V., varsity football players.
2. Give players a fair evaluation before cuts are made. Take into consideration growth and speed potential. Players must feel they have been given a legitimate chance to make the team.
3. Do not be overly concerned about wins. The goal is to start 22 players and allow as many players to participate as possible.

4. Make sure all players have an offensive and defensive position and practice throughout the season at all positions. This should include not just drills but team work.
5. Introduce players to a conditioning routine, including weights.
6. Teach fundamentals and technique. Players must learn how to play the game safely and fairly.
7. Grade checks should be done on a weekly basis.

Parents of Players

Over the course of my 34-year coaching career, I always tried to be up-front and honest with parents, and it eliminated a lot of headaches for me. I always tried to explain our philosophy and how we were trying to make their sons better human beings. I handed out my handbook and mission statement so everybody understood the basic tenants of the program. Then I outlined the schedule and the commitment required so they understood the depth and scope of what they were getting into.

I talked about the cornerstones to our program: accountability, honesty, and how I was asking them and their sons to make a commitment. I always stressed our no drinking or drugs policy, which to me is reason enough to want your son involved with our program. That resonates with parents. I tell them that their sons will make friends and have meaningful relationships without drugs or alcohol being part of it.

They need to know what you're trying to accomplish. I tell them it's not about winning championships but playing at the highest possible level. It would be negligent on our part if we didn't make that attempt—just like it would be negligent for an algebra teacher to teach only two-thirds of the curriculum. If it's too big a commitment for them or their kids, they shouldn't be there. I make that very clear.

I can relate to the concerns of parents because my son, Danny, played for me at De La Salle. (Photo by Bob Larson)

I tell them that if there's 50 kids on the roster, then there's a best player and the 50th best player and I'm equally committed to each and every one in between. I really mean that. No matter where he falls on that scale from one to 50, I promise that we're going to make your son a better football player and a better person.

I tell them they can't help their sons once they step on the field. You may want to, but you can't. They have to figure it out themselves. You can't help them be a better tackler, a better blocker, or a better runner.

Let them succeed or fail. This is something they need to do without parental interference. All you can do is support them and trust us as coaches.

We have an open-door policy, but I want parents to understand that we don't want them fighting their son's battles. Let the kids come see us first and express their concerns. We're not going to belittle them or ignore them. We want to hear it from them—not you. Making sure your voice is heard is an important part of growing up. Don't make excuses for them either. Don't tell me that it was your fault they were late. If they're late, they're late. It doesn't matter. They made a commitment, and you made a commitment.

I also make sure they understand that I have to play the best 11 players. My own son played for me, and he didn't start all the time during his senior year. As much as I wanted him to be a go-to guy, he wasn't always. If I'm willing to do that to my own son, then they should understand that I don't play favorites. I have a responsibility to the whole team and I take that very seriously.

Sometimes parents want me to talk about other kids in the program. I won't do that. It's none of their business. Some parents want to be in the know, almost like they're sitting in on our meetings and game-planning sessions. That's none of their business either. If you're going to let your son do this, you have to trust us to do our jobs.

Sometimes kids have fathers who played and/or coached. They may know the game, but they may also be teaching their kids things we don't agree with. Don't coach them. We're very specific on technique. We know what we want. Let us coach them. Don't coach them yourselves.

Parents often want a status update like, "How is Billy doing?" I avoid this line of questioning because the truth might be: his first step is flat, he's too slow, he's not strong enough, his shoulders are too low, and his hips are too high. If I tell a parent that, they will think I'm negative or being overly critical of their child, even though I'm just being honest. Parents don't always understand that learning the game is a never-ending process.

If there's something going on at home I should know about, I encourage parents to let me know. But I'm not going to meet with them unless their son is also present, as well as his position coach, whenever possible. What I tell a player isn't always what the parents hear. In that case I want the player in the room to clear up any potential miscommunication.

I always have parents contact me via email or my school voicemail. I never give out my personal phone number.

CHAPTER 2

Motivation and Team Building

Creating a team is bigger, tougher, and more elusive than any opponent we will ever face.

—Former De La Salle head coach Bob Ladouceur

Kids and their parents often have unrealistic expectations. They want to compete at a prestigious camp or All-Star Game. They want to play for a major university. They have so many outside things pulling at them, and those outside influences are often concentrated totally on them and nobody else. For that reason it's more difficult to create a team today than it was 20 years ago because kids are pulled in so many different directions. They're always wondering, *What's in it for me? If I put in the time, if I work real hard, will I become a star?*

The first thing I tell kids and their parents is that I don't care about any of that. Creating a team is much more difficult than teaching the game or a specific skill or technique. It's teaching kids how to cooperate with other people. I like to call it being socially sane. Do you have the ability to respect other people and conduct yourself as if the world does not revolve around you and there are other people out there that matter? Can you fit into that mode? It's making kids understand that they must lose some of themselves in order for a team to thrive.

My primary goal is to create an authentic team experience. The game is about creating a team, and that means being unselfish and doing what you're told. It means changing positions if we want you to. It means playing special teams like a demon, being on time, and working hard in the weight room. Don't be a coach watcher. Don't go along for the ride. Don't step back, always step forward. That's why our players set specific individual and unit-by-unit goals every week, including improvement goals, performance goals, and technique goals. Our total and absolute focus is on team. I want them to understand what it means to sacrifice for a team and achieve team-related goals.

They are not it. They are *part* of it.

I've coached players such as Amani Toomer, Aaron Taylor, and Maurice Jones-Drew who have gone on to successful careers in college and the NFL. We treated them exactly the same as everybody else. We won't stand for any selfish behavior, regardless of how talented a player might be. As it turned out, those guys were our hardest workers, but any kid who comes into our program and thinks maybe he could be a Division I guy, we make sure he knows he is working for the team.

It's the here and now that we're concerned with. We'll help you and promote you if you deserve it, if you prove you are a team guy. That's where your priority has to be. This is not about you. This is about you playing for the guy making all your blocks, opening the holes you run through, and giving you time to complete or catch a pass. It's about playing for the guy who is taking on blockers so you can make the tackles.

We get good results that way. Our guys turn into good team guys. Even our best players have been great in terms of being leaders and captains—being first in our conditioning drills and the hardest workers in the weight room. It's because we insist on it. It's the only way you can create a team atmosphere. We don't play favorites. We don't coddle anybody.

Kids want to be good at something. When they come out for football, they want to be good at it. The motivation is different for every kid. Some kids love the game and want to compete, some kids like contact (not many, but some). Some kids want to be popular, want to be an athlete. They want to wear their jacket around. It's an identity. Then you have guys who want to be around a team and aren't really interested in starting and exceling, but they enjoy the companionship of playing. You get all sorts of kids who play for different reasons. That hasn't changed. It might be a little different nowadays because sometimes kids play for athletic scholarships or because they have visions of playing in the NFL. When I played I wanted to do something not everybody else could do. It gave me a sense of pride that I was doing something unnatural, difficult, something a lot of people didn't like to do.

I believe team is personality driven beginning with the individual. Are you a team guy? Do you know what it means to be a teammate? Do you know what it means to be a fully functioning member of a team? As much as we've worked on kids and tried to turn them and we can turn them sometimes and bring them around, there are others who are unwilling to be teammates. They're not meant to be. I've never found the formula to be able to turn some of those guys.

One of them in particular was a player I'll call "Michael." Every team has a Michael or multiple Michaels. Michael wasn't a team guy. He questioned everything whether he believed it or not. He was always somewhat stubborn and didn't want to change. His humor was cruel. He didn't get along with kids. He loved to put kids down. He wasn't funny. He thought he was, but he wasn't. I wanted to change this kid somehow. The way we do that is by bringing him into our office, sitting him down, and telling him our concerns. I might say, "Look, this is what you're doing, this is how you are. This is not working on our team. It's detrimental to our unity."

His answer was, "That's just the way I am. That's just my personality."

I said, "That's really unfortunate because you just shut the door on change, and change is good, and we all must change. We all have to evolve. We all have to adjust. We all have to grow. Change is growth. You just shut the door on growth and change. You don't want to do that."

Those are the guys who hurt your team, hurt your program. They drag it down. They find other guys who feel the same way and they create divisions. You can't turn everybody, but the wisest people are those who are willing to understand their shortcomings, work on them, admit their wrongdoings, and move forward from there.

The ones who can't be turned into team guys have to go to maintain the integrity of the whole. We have cut guys who have been phenomenal players or could have been phenomenal players, but they just couldn't fit into a team concept. They were late to practice or they always had excuses for why they couldn't be there. We are always fine without players like that because our program is based around a commitment we all make to each other, which serves as our ultimate motivation.

We become stronger in the absence of a player, however talented, who doesn't share our commitment.

» DISCIPLINE

I used to hand parents a sheet of paper with 20 rules that could get their son in trouble. On a few occasions, I had parents play lawyer with me. *The rule says he's not supposed to be drinking. He was seen holding a beer, but nobody saw him sipping from it…He was passing the joint to another person. He wasn't smoking it…He had a cooler of beer in the trunk of his car, but it wasn't for him. It was for his friends who weren't football players.*

That's when I did away with the rules.

If you lie, cheat, or steal around school, in your car, at home, or on the street, you're violating team rules. If you drink alcohol or use drugs, tobacco products, or unapproved supplements, you're in violation of team rules, period. If you sass a teacher or are disrespectful, we'll mete out a fair punishment for that, too.

If you don't like it, too bad. That's the way we do things.

When my students do something wrong or break a rule and come back and say, "I didn't know. I wasn't aware that was the wrong thing to do." I'm like, "Come on. How many of us do wrong things and really don't know it's wrong? Be honest. Own your baggage. Everything usually turns out better from that point anyway." Every time I did something wrong, I knew it was wrong and I did it anyway. So, when they use those excuses: "I didn't do anything wrong." That's not an acceptable answer.

I tell parents we operate in the best interest of your son. If your son is hurting the integrity of the team, he's going to pay the price for it. That will be a lesson in itself. We want to do what's in the best interest of the team and what's in the best interest of your son as well.

We're fair. We're consistent. We're not going to cut people off at the ankles. If a player back sasses a teacher, and it's not that serious or if it's the first time, we'll give him a warning. That's it. Next time you sit for a half or miss a game. No excuses. If a kid takes a swing at somebody, that's automatic. He sits. Same thing if he gets caught drinking or smoking. That's one game regardless of who next week's opponent is or where we are in our season.

You have to be alcohol and drug-free to be a Spartan. I tell parents their sons will improve dramatically as football players, they will learn to embrace fitness, and they will build lifelong friendships. They will be around other great kids and they will do a lot of things together and have a lot of fun. They'll laugh, they'll bond, they'll learn to depend on each other, and there won't be a drop of alcohol involved.

I would want my child to participate for that reason alone. I would want him to be a member of that club. That's a major bonus for parents. Kids might be worried about playing time, but they should be thankful for everything else they get out of it: friendship, lifestyle, camaraderie, and discipline.

Assistant coaches can be more fraternal with players, but a head coach must tread a fine line. You can't have the same relationship with your players that their peers have with them. That's not your job. You're an adult. They're kids. They already have friends. They need you as a coach, a mentor, an expert, a teacher, somebody they know will hold them accountable and discipline them. They definitely have to see you as a father figure, but you're not going to kill them with love unless it's tough love.

I told the kids every year: "I'm not going to be your friend, your buddy. I'm going to do my job and teach you how to play football. I'm going to hold you accountable for your actions and teach you how to play the game and assess you in all those areas. If you're not doing what we expect you to do, there will be consequences."

They need that framework. Most child psychologists believe that kids need boundaries. They need to know how far they can push and when they cross the line. There's that element to it. I'm not a professional coach. They can be a little more lax. They can cut players. If they have a bad apple, they can trade them. These are kids. You're trying to mold them. You're preparing them for life. Being a high school coach is a different job.

Modern coaches don't like confronting kids and holding them accountable. It's uncomfortable. Sitting kids down, calling their parents—that's the least fun part of the job, and a lot of coaches avoid it. We don't. When we hear rumors, we pursue them because they are usually correct. We understand the culture. We seek out information.

We had a quarterback a few years ago with a maturity problem. He was one of those kids who took advantage of substitute teachers by acting out in class. We talked to him about it. We warned him. I was in the lunch room one day and heard a substitute teacher talking about how everyone in her class was throwing spit wads. I asked if the quarterback was in the class. She said he was. I asked where he was sitting. She said he was sitting in the back left corner. I went to the classroom and found a snowdrift of spit wads in the back left corner of the room and suspended my starting quarterback for that week's game.

We don't let stuff slide. Our kids know it, too. They know if they do something wrong they're going to be caught. A lot of young coaches don't want to do that, but that's part of creating a team. If you play favorites or you won't sit your star athlete when it's appropriate to do so, the kids lose respect for you. They can recognize a double standard. I've suspended a starter for the first quarter of the first game because he had trouble in the classroom during the offseason. After a warning the player made another disrespectful comment toward his teacher. Then he threw a piece of paper at the garbage and missed. The teacher asked him to pick it up, and he said that was BS.

This was a school matter. We could've let the dean handle it, but he was also part of our team. We expect discipline to reach all aspects of their lives. I don't personally believe you can be a total flake in life and then get out on a football field and all of a sudden put it all together. If you pay any attention to the news, that's being proven on a daily basis.

When we talk about discipline, we're talking about discipline throughout the whole program throughout the whole year. If you're a Spartans football player, you're accountable and responsible to our team 24 hours a day, seven days a week, 365 days per year, on and off the field. That's critical to our program.

Coaches aren't doing athletes any favors by letting them get away with things because of their athletic ability or because they need them to win that week's game. Police blotters are filled with guys who received that treatment. Do you think the coaches of athletes who find themselves in serious trouble later in life did them any favors by letting their behavior slide? Do you think the college and pro athletes who find themselves on the police blotters would've benefitted from tough lessons when they were in high school? There have to be consequences for poor behavior. How can you prepare someone for life if he never gets punished because he's a good athlete?

We want our players to understand that being a Spartans football player isn't about football as much as it is about life and being a caring, empathetic individual. That's real important to us. We feel that accountability carries onto the field, knowing that's who you are as a person. It's one of the greatest life lessons they can learn. When they do mess up—and they're teenagers so they almost always do—they have to be disciplined.

Benching a third-stringer is easy. Benching a starter hurts, and we make the player and his parents and the team aware of that. But we're willing to hurt the team to teach the lesson that what you do affects the entire team and not just yourself. A lot of coaches aren't willing, and that only feeds the negative behavior that leads to the kind of arrests and embarrassments that have become all too common in sports today.

» LEADERSHIP

Good teams don't have one or two good leaders but multiple good leaders. One or two aren't going to pull you through or carry you. There is no such thing as one or two guys carrying a team.

Now think about the terms "leader" and "follower." Automatically we think leader is positive and follower is negative, but it's the quality of your character and your personality that infuses those words with meaning. We're all followers at times. I'm a follower, too. I have bosses. I have to do what they want me to do and be a part of the program and get into lockstep with what they want.

Then we think of a follower and we think of them as mindless. They can't make up their own mind and can't make their own decisions. Every team needs great followers, too, guys who do the work, get behind the ideas, and believe in what they're doing. You have to believe in what you're following and what people stand for when you're working toward it. All my great teams had multiple team leaders, and many of them started out as followers. I don't believe in natural-born leaders. To me, that's a myth. Leadership is a skill learned through experience.

For example, we always seem to have a group of five or six seniors who are self-starters. They run and lift and do all the months of prep work and they will do it 100 percent every minute of every day. Then we have new guys on the team who we feel could be really good players, but they are lazy, don't have a work ethic, and are trying to figure it out. The senior self-starters will stick together and so will the young guys. We break those groups up. We put the new guys with the self-starters, and they make the young guys put more weight on the bar. They will move those guys through the program and teach them how to work.

Don't confuse a charismatic personality with a good leader. There's a lot of quiet, introverted, good leaders. Being charismatic can assist you as a leader, but it's not essential for leadership either. I'm an introvert.

Every Myers-Briggs exam I ever took or psychological makeup I ever have done always rates me as an introvert on an extreme scale. I get freaked out before I get in front of people. That's part of my DNA. It's something that has always been a part of me for my entire life.

You have to be yourself. I'm that introvert. I'm that quiet guy. Coach Eidson calls me one of the most boring guys in the world. That's not too far from the truth. I'm not a real exciting guy, but I work with what I have because any attempts at not being yourself fail miserably. I had some guys who were great guys, friendly, outgoing, nice guys, good teachers. Then they got onto the football field and became raging maniacs because they were emulating some coach they may have had in their own Pop Warner or high school days. I'm like, "What are you doing? You come out here and you're totally not who you are."

You have to be who you are and teach these guys through your own personality. You don't have to rant and rave if that's not who you are. Kids will see through that. You can't switch your personality on and off like that. Then nobody knows who they are going to have to deal with that day. Be yourself.

The Power of a Commitment

If I had to choose one thing a student-athlete learned from playing for me, it would be how to make a commitment. These commitments extend to all facets of life. Wherever I go or whatever I do, I carry that commitment with me, knowing I'm connected to a group who loves, accepts, and respects me but will also hold me accountable for my actions on-and-off the field, 365 days a year, 24 hours a day.

No exceptions, no excuses.

It means answering to 45 teammates, following rules, and understanding individual attitudes and actions affect the whole. This commitment is an enormous responsibility. It means I am going to expect the best from you, and you can expect the best from me. It's not enough to show up, go along for the ride, or look the other way when we see a teammate doing less than his best. It's not the commitment itself, but the *degree* of our commitment that makes our program unique.

It's not enough to say we work. We don't go through the motions or satisfy ourselves with the minimum expected. Our players know the pain and dedication necessary to ready their bodies for top-flight athletic competition. We as coaches know those grueling hours spent in the weight room or pulling tires across the sun-bleached grass every summer is what galvanizes our players into a team greater than the sum of its parts.

That commitment is not an assumption but a promise that I will be there for you and I can count on you being there for me. From the way you spot my barbell to the effort you give on a double-team block to the lift home you give a teammate after practice, being able to honestly say "I was there for you" is one of the most difficult and rewarding commitments our players will make and comes closest to plumbing the true depth of our humanity.

That may be as close as I can come to describing the key to our success. Teams that accept the commitment play their best football down the stretch. It's inspiring to see. Teams that don't make that commitment to each other struggle. That's why as coaches we are as demanding about players holding each other accountable as anything we do on the field.

» MOTIVATION

I don't believe in pregame speeches just as I believe much of the so-called emotion often associated with football is meaningless to begin with. That's why I don't try to fire up kids before a game. I don't let my coaches or other players do it either. Genuine motivation comes from within. In my mind, if players need to be fired up or if coaches believe that's necessary, they are in deep trouble before the game even starts. When I see an opposing team charge out of the locker room whooping and hollering, I always figure we're in pretty good shape. Kids should feel confident and committed when they take the field, but I don't want them banging heads and screaming in each other's faces. I want to see resolve.

I've always thought motivation was real overblown. It's all window dressing. Real motivation is teaching a kid a skill. When they start mastering those skills and begin to have success in practice, they become excited and now they really want to play. Now they know they can go against somebody bigger and faster and defeat them. We've had scores of kids that do that every year. My guy is 6'1", 210 pounds, and he's playing against a Division-I guy who weighs 260 and he'll have success because he knows his technique and is getting off the ball and into his opponent or striking him on defense or getting into his gap and taking care of his responsibilities—not because he worked himself into a froth before the game.

Thursday Night Team Meetings

My teams struggled early in games during my first three years as a head coach. They were getting pushed around, and I couldn't figure out why.

My high school coach invited players to his house for ice cream and to review the gameplan the night before games, so I started doing the same during the 1982 season. That was the first of my 29 undefeated teams. Over the next few years, dessert evolved into full-fledged meals, and team dinners became a cornerstone of our success.

Thursday night team meals are also a great way to get parents involved. Parents want to feel like they're included and they are on these nights. They also get to see the team in a social setting. If you're doing your job as coaches, parents will come away impressed because players will be polite, gracious, and responsible. We make sure our kids thank the host family as well as the parents who prepared the meal and cleaned up afterward.

The dinner itself is a social event that allows players to interact outside of the school setting. I want to hear laughter and kids having fun together during the meal. As coaches, we do the same thing. The mood doesn't get serious until we begin the actual meeting, which usually takes place in the garage with the door closed, so parents can't hear snippets of conversation that may be taken out of context. Since we don't have pregame talks, Thursday night's meetings are our last chance to prepare our players for the game. The first thing we do is break into position groups, so coaches can go through their checklists for the upcoming game.

That checklist often involves the opposing team's personnel and tendencies and how we plan to counter. A quarterback may talk about how he's supposed to react when he sees various defenses, for example, while a linebacker should know what to expect when one of the opposing team's best offensive players lines up in a specific formation. I want the kids to know their responsibilities, know their opponent, and be able to talk about what they're going to do and what they anticipate. When all the checklists are done, I usually address the team, though sometimes other coaches might talk, too, especially if I think the team needs a different voice. Then I turn the meeting over to the players.

In the early years, when I was trying to get the kids talking, I started asking them how they personally felt about the game emotionally, and they would say things like, "This is a critical game for us," and it eventually became even more personal. I'd ask, "What are you going to do in the game tomorrow? What's one of your goals?" They would talk about how they needed someone else's help. The quarterback might stand up and say, "If you give me time to throw, I'll hit that pass we practiced all week or that route we've been working on." Then it turned into players talking about what they needed to do collectively and how they depended on each other, which I loved.

I don't want them talking to me. I want them all talking to *each other* about what they need to do. Thursday night meetings often become very emotional—from kids tearfully promising to improve their play to make their teammates better to discussing what problems they might be having at home or at school.

Their performance means more to them because they realize they are connected to something bigger, that they aren't playing just for themselves, that their execution affects everybody else. As a result, it's rare for a player to spend two years in our program without becoming emotional in front of his teammates at a Thursday night meeting. If you're going to play here, you must be willing to stand in front of your teammates and cry.

We try to make our football team a place where a player is safe to be his authentic self, the best self he can be. We work hard to break down

Our Thursday night meetings are an integral part of forging the special bonds that exist between the players on our team. (Photo by Bob Larson)

walls such as race, religion, jealousy, hate, and social status so we can experience each other on a truly human level, and that's never more prominent than at the end of Thursday night meetings.

It doesn't always happen right away. Some teams feel that connection immediately, and others don't discover it until middle or even late in the season. It doesn't matter *when* it happens as long as it *does* happen, though I can tell you from experience, the teams that feel that close connection and freely share their feelings and emotions have absolutely been our best teams on the field. There is a direct correlation between how much they care about each other and how well they play together.

The 2004 team that had our 151-game winning streak snapped and is portrayed in the film version of *When the Game Stands Tall* is a perfect example. That was one of our least talented teams, but it was also fractured. That group was immature, lacked senior leadership, and didn't get along with each other but still felt entitled. Because they wore the De La Salle uniform, they believed they deserved to keep the winning streak alive even if they didn't fully understand how to practice and prepare. It was no surprise to me when after 151 consecutive victories we started the 2004 season 0–2–1.

Around midseason they started figuring it out, the meetings became more emotional, and by the end of the year, that team had maximized its potential as well as any team we've had here. For that reason and despite the 12 straight undefeated seasons that preceded it, that team was not a disappointment in my mind. It reached its utmost potential.

When the kids talk during our Thursday night meetings, I just listen and correct them when they need it. An emotional kid might say something hyperbolic like, "I just want you guys to know, I'd die out on that field for you." While I appreciate the sentiment, I make sure they keep things in perspective. I might say something like, "No one is going to die. It's only high school football." Another thing kids often say is, "We're going to look back on this night as the greatest time of our lives." Again, I understand where they're coming from, but I try to get them to keep the right mind-set. "Just so you know, you guys are young, and if this ends up being the greatest night of your lives, you will have lived sad lives," I tell them.

One of the most important things we can do as coaches is teach kids that there's more to life than high school football. I don't let our kids stand up in our Thursday night meeting and talk about how we are going to do this or that. You can't speak for anyone else because you don't know what he is going to do. You only know what *you* are going to do so you can only speak for yourself.

Commitment Cards

Steve Alexakos, my former offensive line coach, came up with the idea for commitment cards, and it was so effective with his unit that we involved the whole team and incorporated it into our Thursday night meetings. It has become perhaps our most effective motivational tool because it encourages kids to be accountable to each other.

Every week players must write down one practice goal, one conditioning goal, and one game goal on a white index card. During Thursday night's team meeting, players stand up and not only state their goals but commit them to a teammate or coach who is then responsible for holding that player accountable. Players can't commit to the same teammate twice, which eliminates cliques and forces players to interact with more than just a few teammates.

After films on Saturday, commitment card partners stand up and re-read the goals before telling the team whether or not the goals were reached. The key is that the goals have to be measurable and realistic. A player can't say, "I'm going to play as hard as I can," for example. That's not a measurable goal. An offensive lineman can't say he's going to get his first step right 100 percent of the time if he has never accomplished it 40 percent of the time before. Making that kind of jump is not realistic. A starting running back, on the other hand, may commit to finishing in the top three in gassers after practice that week as his conditioning goal, having 100 percent ball security in practice, and rushing for 115 yards in the upcoming game because those goals are measureable.

On Saturday, after watching film, we go over the commitments from the previous week. The teammate with the running back's commitment card might stand up and announce that the running back did finish in the top three in gassers, but he fumbled in practice and had only 74 yards in the game. Then we might ask that running back, "You haven't achieved your commitments for three weeks. What's going on?" His teammates are listening. They want answers, too. It's not just coaches holding him accountable but his teammates, too, and that's powerful. Our players monitor each other, encourage each other to accomplish their goals, and hold each other accountable when they don't.

What I like most about commitment cards is they are all-inclusive. If we have 50 kids on the roster, there's the best player and the 50th best player, and everybody else falls somewhere in between. We want our kids to know, wherever they fall in that spectrum, they are accountable to each other. Earlier in my career, I noticed my team would split into two camps: the kids who knew they were going to play and the kids who knew they weren't going to play much. The key contributors were motivated and pushing each other to get better while the kids who knew they weren't going to play went to the back of the pack. They stood around and watched and often became whiners or complainers. I had to beg them to do drill work.

Commitment cards changed that because even if they weren't going to play, they had to make a conditioning commitment and a practice commitment. Suddenly, those guys were engaged. Our scout-team guys often give their commitment cards to the starters they practice against every day, and all of those guys get better. If a backup defensive back commits to deflecting three passes in practice during the week, it will increase the intensity and make the players he's playing against work that much harder. When everybody is competing to reach their goals, practices take on more gameday intensity, which is beneficial to everybody.

We even had a player who was getting dominated in practice say he was only going to get flat-backed twice in practice that week. Everybody laughed, but I thought that was a great goal. It was his way of telling his teammates that he was never going to quit fighting. I promise parents at the beginning of every season that everybody on the roster will become a better football player. Nobody is going to get disenchanted. They are going to participate, they are going to set goals, and they are going to be evaluated by their peers every week, and commitment cards are a big part of that.

The way we take the field has become our signature. We do so two-by-two with our players holding hands in a show of unity. What most people don't realize is players are paired with their commitment card partner, which just reinforces the accountability we demand and the bonds it creates. What I didn't realize until years later was that most players have kept their commitment cards, which tells me how much they mean to them. We have even had players elevate the concept by making lifetime commitments to each other and holding each other accountable, which shows what a positive motivational tool the cards can be—not only on the football field but beyond.

||||||||||||||||||||||||||||||||||||||||||||||||||||||||||||||||||||||||||||||||||||||||||||||||||||

Chapel Service

By De La Salle defensive and special teams coordinator Terry Eidson

De La Salle is a Catholic school, and one of our goals is to develop our players spiritually, which is the primary reason we started holding chapel services on Thursday afternoons. We know praying and quoting scripture won't fly at most public schools, but there's still value in kids relaxing in a quiet environment during a hectic week of school and football.

Our kids lie on our chapel's carpeted floor after school on Thursdays. A typical service lasts 45 minutes. Some may wonder why we have a prayer service on Thursday afternoon and a team meetings on Thursday nights. Because we encourage kids to share their emotions at both, you might think it's redundant. We don't look at it that way.

We talk more about improving ourselves as people instead of football players during chapel service. When kids do talk, it's more about their relationships with their teammates and what may be happening in their lives off the field. Team meetings are more focused on details of the game, though that can also often result in more discussions about relationships.

Every chapel service has a theme. Challenging yourself, a willingness to risk it all, or the toughness of the game might be themes depending on where we are as a team. What it means to make a commitment, being all-in, and becoming better friends and teammates are other common themes.

I teach religious studies. Coach Ladouceur did for years, too. I was always the one who organized the chapel services. I start by playing a song that introduces that week's theme. Players are given lyrics so they can better understand how the song relates. When the song ends, I introduce the theme and talk about why it was chosen before supporting it by reading scripture, a poem, or some other brief passage from a book or magazine that supports the theme. I may even download something from the Internet if it supports the chosen theme.

I only organize the first couple chapel services before making players responsible for choosing themes, picking out appropriate songs and readings, and making sure everybody has copies. We encourage the players to talk after the readings. Sometimes they do, and sometimes they don't. Usually, a kid will talk about the theme and how it relates to him. He might say, "I really like this reading because I think I need to challenge myself more," or "Sometimes I don't have enough confidence in myself and I need to play with more confidence." We've had kids say, "This reading reminds me why I love being on this team because you guys are always there for me, and I feel everyone is committed to something and I've never felt that before." A player who is struggling with off-the-field issues might say, "I appreciate the way you guys have been there for me while my grandfather is in the hospital."

Sometimes I'm amazed and totally inspired by what kids talk about during chapel and at Thursday night meetings, and sometimes I'm totally uninspired. They're teenagers. You never know what's going to happen next.

When the seniors feel everybody has come together as one, they bring chain links to symbolize how a team is only as strong as its weakest link. Whether that happens in Week 4 or Week 10, that's always a powerful service, as is the last service of the year, when seniors have two minutes each for their "last thoughts" before their high school football careers end. We end chapel service with a community prayer and then we offer each other the sign of peace, which we define as a hug. The kids will literally circle the room, saying, "Peace be with you," and hugging each other one by one to symbolize our brotherhood and commitment to each other. We listen to a final reflection song before ending the service.

Feedback

At the core of my coaching philosophy is direct feedback and being honest with players about their talents, what they're capable of, and what their potential is. You can't fool kids. They see much more than most people give them credit for. High school kids are at an age when they are trying to figure out who they are and who they want to become, so they are constantly scrutinizing adults around them, looking for fakes, identifying hypocrisy, gauging sincerity.

Kids want to be treated like adults and they are capable of incredible achievements when thus empowered. They will rise up to meet challenges many would not believe them capable of when they are given honest—sometimes even painfully honest—feedback. I might say, "Look, you are loafing," or "You're not living up to your potential. You could be so much more than you are." It resonates with them. It rocks a lot of kids to the core, as well it should, because growth is only possible when we take a hard look at ourselves and ask ourselves the really tough questions. Am I really giving it my best? Am I cutting corners? Can I be better than I am?

Young athletes have to really see themselves before they grow. I've tried to be that mirror for them. Our staff remains very good at that. We're always giving them the feedback they need to hear, and 80 percent of it is negative feedback. Sometimes outsiders think we're down on kids, and we're not bolstering them and giving them confidence. We take the opposite philosophy. We're not going to lie to kids. We're going to tell them, "Your game is not good right now, and here's why it's not good—you take a lateral step or a drop step. Your hips are too high or your base is too wide."

I've had coaches in the past who I overheard telling players, "You got beat. Do it again. That's not good enough." That means nothing. That means they are going to do it again and get beat again. You can't coach for me if that's how you approach it. If that happens, the coach should get them back in line and say, "Look, you took a side step, you got your feet outside his frame, your head was down, you turned your shoulder."

Whatever it is, the feedback you give to help him perform that task has to be nonstop vigilance all the time. That's why we go home at night and we're totally exhausted. We're like, "Man, what a day. We stunk." You're so tired because you're concentrating and watching these guys nonstop all the time. It is two-and-a-half hours of complete concentration and work. You can't take any plays off. You don't want to beat the tar out of your kids in team work so you have to make every play count. You've got to watch them as closely and efficiently as possible. It's the same with their drill work. You don't want a kid going up there and doing a live drill and not getting any feedback—positive or negative. I've had coaches who sit there in practice and don't say a word. That's not coaching. Whether it's good or bad, give them feedback so they know what they're doing.

Developing Players

If I were to describe our coaching style, it would be one day at a time. I know that sounds like a cliché, but we get our kids together and think about what we're going to do that day to challenge them so when they're coming off the field they will be in better shape and they will be one step closer to doing what they're supposed to be doing and putting it all together.

We coach every kid and we develop our younger guys, too, because we know that sophomore who isn't any good or that junior who is horrible will probably be starting for us next year if we stay with him. That's a big part of our success. Virtually every year we'll have five starters who have never started a varsity football game until they became seniors. Those guys will play great football for us. We stick with them, and they wake up during the offseason before their senior season and they start lifting like crazy. They grow. They get bigger and faster and already know what we want and what's expected. They step in and start doing great stuff. Not all of them but a lot of them. It's a developmental step for us. We develop all our guys right on through, and it always comes back to that drill work.

When we've got a defensive lineman, we're going to teach him his one and three-technique and how to defeat a blocker and how to cover his responsibility and get him to hustle and make plays he's not supposed to make. We do that for every player on our team. We're going to make them better football players. I tell players this: "The way we coach is we invest in you. You're going to improve as the season goes on, and by the time we get to the playoffs, there's no doubt you're going to be doing your jobs and doing them well, and that will result in success for us."

That's why we often struggle early in the year. These guys don't have their technique down. They're not getting off blocks. They're standing up too high, they're not pass-blocking well because their feet aren't underneath them, and they're too spread out. Kids don't know what they're capable of. We know what they're capable of and we know it when we see it, so we keep harping on them until we get what we want from them, and that can mean 12 or 13 weeks of us being on their case.

We turn the responsibility and success of the team over to the kids midway through the season. We say, "Look, we've coached you for six months since January, and now it's October. Either you guys do this stuff, or we all go down together. It's your turn. You've been coached enough. You know what you're supposed to do. You know your responsibilities. We're not going to stop coaching you, but you pick up the slack now. You carry the team through right to the end." They have to do that. They have to mature as the season goes.

Sometimes a kid can't do what we expect him to, and at the end of the season, we'll say, "Well, I guess he couldn't do it." But we won't give up on him. We're going to fix his technique, and by the end of the year through repetition and one-on-ones and doing the same thing day after tedious, monotonous day, he's going to be a better player than he ever thought he could be. We train our players to peak in the last game of the season, which is the state championship game. So when they line up against those elite athletes—and there are a lot of elite athletes on the field in the state title game—they will be prepared for it.

When they dominate an average guy during the season, we tell them it's because they should have. That's expected. But there are guys down the road who aren't going to be like that guy. Yeah, we want to win these games and play well, but you're trained for something way bigger than this. We let them know that when they get into the playoffs they're going to face opponents equal to their ability or better. Our guys rise to the challenge.

Talking to the Team

I never say anything to kids that I don't myself believe and I don't ask them to do anything that I don't do. That's important. In my opinion the relationship between a coach and his players starts with that. What we tried to do with our kids was accelerate the adult maturation process. We want to make these guys adults quicker and introduce them to the adult world faster than most kids their age so we hold them to an incredibly high standard. When you get a team with players who behave like adults, they are usually unbelievably good. They understand a lot more.

To get to that level, you have to hold them to a consistent standard of mature, adult behavior, and I want them to understand why we do that, too. I don't want it to be reward and punishment. I want them to think at a higher level of human development. They want to treat their teammate well because it's the human thing to do, the right thing to do, the moral thing to do, not because they will get punished if they don't.

If you want them to behave like adults, you have to talk to them like adults. I'm very honest and up-front with them. I say, "I've coached the game for more than 30 years. My experience can help you. My job is to give you feedback on how you're performing. Here's what we did well today, here's what we didn't do well, and here's what we have to improve on tomorrow." I always avoid generalities because the kids don't know if they apply to them or not. For example, you can say, "You're not hustling." Most kids will shrug and think: *I'm hustling.*

Blanket statements are meaningless. I might say, "Our offense was spotty today. It wasn't good. Gibbons, you fumbled twice. Brookings ran the wrong route twice, Johnson dropped two passes, Harmon didn't pick up the blitz. The offensive line got no movement. Smith, your side was a tire fire. Peterson and Martinez, you were not tough last week. You didn't get any sacks, you got stood up, you failed to win the neutral zone."

It might seem harsh, but I wouldn't say it if it weren't true. Serving as a mirror for our players is a huge, huge part of our success. We know what we want and need to see and we recognize it when we see it in real time, and that's what makes us good coaches, and our kids understand that. The only way we're going to get what we want is to provide feedback. I consider that my No. 1 job.

CHAPTER 3

Practicing, Scouting, and Gameplanning

Teams stick pretty close to what they've done in the past. They usually stay true to their tendencies.

—Former De La Salle head coach Bob Ladouceur

One of my faults is disorganization. I'm organized in my mind but disorganized on paper. I don't type well. Computers hate me. I was real fortunate to surround myself with guys who could manage my disorganization. For example, during my 34 years as head coach, I never used a practice plan. Instead, we gathered in the coaches' office 10 minutes before practice and I would ask every coach, "How much time do you need?"

If Coach Eidson feels the defensive backs aren't doing the job, he will make sure the defensive backs coach is addressing that. If receivers aren't running their routes right, I might tell the receivers coach to make an adjustment. We're pretty autonomous. I might say, "Let's get together at 4:00 PM for teamwork." That's it. They will have a 45-minute block at the beginning of practice to do what they need to do and they know what needs to be done. They know the gameplan. They know what plays we want to run, what we want to concentrate on, and what they feel they need to get better at during drill work.

I was not one of those coaches who let things slide when they're not going right. If we weren't executing, I would keep working on it until we got it right. If we started executing well and then things started getting shabby, we'd had enough. It was time to move on. If things started out shabby, I always tried to resurrect it as best I could. I never wanted the kids to think we could stink in practice and that was okay. It's not okay. I'm not one to say, "We don't have it for whatever reason. Let's call it a day." That's not how it works. I would stick with it until they got it right. I won't let it go and hope they do it right during the game. If it's not working initially, I'm going to try to make it work, so sometimes those individual periods at the beginning of practice got lengthened or shortened.

If I felt like I needed 10 more minutes, our coaches were talented enough to adjust. They all know there are things they could work on. As a coach you always have something in the back of your mind to work on when you get a chance. I might say, "I want to work the run game today," or "I want to work on these four or five plays." Coach

Alumbaugh, Coach Eidson, and the guys would say, "That will take 20 minutes during individual and 20 during group work." That was it. That's how we worked stuff out. I might be involved in something where I'm halfway through it and remember, *Oh, yeah, we're supposed to be in team work right now.* Or one of the coaches would yell across the field, "When's team work?" I might say, "Give me 10 more minutes." That's the only practice plan we ever used.

I've seen college and pro coaches who have a horn going off every five minutes, and guys running all over the field. That can work, too, I guess, but I don't see it as essential. Maybe their playbooks are so vast they have to break it down that way. We're not that extensive. We're basic. The popular trend today is keep the kids moving and never do the same thing twice. When I hear an opposing coach has that philosophy, I know we're in good shape because we do the same things over and over and over again until they become second nature, part of who we are.

I never run a drill without someone snapping to the quarterback. Whether it's seven on seven, a ballhandling drill, or individual group work, we call a cadence and snap the ball to the quarterback because you have to have that timing. Any drill you work has got to have some kind of game-related element to it or you're just spinning your wheels.

The only real difference between our fall practices and our summer workouts is they're wearing pads. The drills stay the same. The practice time and schedule stay the same. During the first week of the season, we're just trying to get kids accustomed to doing drill work in pads and we're trying to teach them how to hit and move people and to be aggressive. That's a good time to watch the young guys and see how much they have progressed during the summer and how much they can help you once the season begins. The returners who have proven themselves get less work during that first week because we know what they can do. We start involving them more during the second week so they are as prepared as possible for the first game.

How quickly we can install our offense, defense, and special teams depends on how experienced the team is and how quickly they pick up things. Some years you can be more exotic because we have a lot of returning players. Other years we have to spend more time on basic veer plays to build muscle memory. Hopefully, their focus will increase as that first game approaches. They should sense the urgency. The kids can hear it in our voices. Everyone can feel it as the game approaches. Things are getting real.

Tempo

I've never been a proponent of walk-throughs or asking kids to perform at less than 100 percent. Ask kids to go 60 percent and you won't get game-like tempo or energy. Besides, when you say, "We're going 70 percent today," kids don't even know what that means. One kid might go hard while another goes slower. The linemen might go 50 percent and the running backs 80 percent.

It never works. It throws the timing off-kilter.

We want to have up-tempo practices because kids lose interest and concentration during down time and because that's how we play in games. We absolutely correct mistakes in real time on the practice field, but it shouldn't take two or three minutes. Every coach is responsible for watching his area and his area only. Coach Alumbaugh might yell at a guard, "Your first step was six inches too long." Coach Panella might tell the quarterback that his first step was outside the frame, but we do that while they are returning to the huddle, so we can maintain tempo.

Our practice production changed dramatically when video coordinator Tony DeMattei started filming practices several years ago. What a difference it makes. Our practices are 15 to 20 minutes shorter because we don't have to get on the ball and do a lot of talking. We can go up-tempo and, though we still correct the kids in real time, we also watch the film with the kids the next day at lunch.

We run at least three plays a minute. To do that you have to rotate guys, but we try to get as many reps as we can to as many players as possible. We've found the kids make fewer mistakes when we go up-tempo. It forces them to be focused and engaged. If they stand around for two or three minutes, run a play, and then stand around again, practice gets too long. It gets boring. We want them captivated and we want them physically taxed afterward.

||||||||||||||||||||||||||||||||||||||||||||||||||||||||||||||||||||||||||||||||||||||||||||||||||||||||||||

One on Ones

By former De La Salle head coach Bob Ladouceur and current De La Salle head coach Justin Alumbaugh

Our one on ones are the heart and soul of our program. It involves one offensive lineman and one defensive lineman both trying to win the neutral zone. It improves their skills, their steps, and their contact points. Eventually, we want our offensive linemen to get to a point where they can block one on one and not rely on double-teams or tandem blocks. We want our defensive linemen to keep those offensive linemen on the line of scrimmage and defeat their blockers and clog running lanes. It's a season-long process for both groups and it unfolds during one-on-one drills every Monday and Wednesday. Football is about defeating the man in front of you. Everything else plays out from there.

We try to match up size versus size, skill versus skill, starters versus starters. The kids want it that way. They learn how to challenge each other. Rivalries and competitive attitudes are created. We film them, too, and watch them with the kids during lunch.

We have three lines of defensive linemen and three lines of offensive linemen. When one group finishes and we blow the whistle, the next group should be in their stances and ready to go because we want to run them quickly. If a kid has a complete failure, we usually give him another shot at it. The coach stands behind the defensive lineman and he holds up fingers to represent the snap count and then he points in the direction he wants the offensive lineman to attempt to block the defensive linemen.

When the ball is snapped, the offensive and defensive line coaches are mostly looking at feet but also pad level and points of contact. A lot of kids like to step sideways, but when you do that, you get beat. Both guys want to win the neutral zone, and whoever does will have success.

The one-on-one drills during practice are the heart of our program.
(Photo by Bob Larson)

‖‖‖

Hitting

By former De La Salle head coach Bob Ladouceur

I don't like having a guy on the team who won't pay the pain price. That doesn't have anything to do with lifting weights or running on the track either. *I want them to work past the fear of getting hit.* That's the price you have to pay to be part of the club. You have to accept the pain initiation and overcome that fear of getting hit because that's the essence of the game. That is the game. If you let a kid go through your program without challenging him in that way, you've cheated him.

Most of the kids who don't want to hit aren't going to start or play much anyway, but if you want to call yourself a De La Salle football player, you have to do that. It may take them a long time, but eventually they will come around and start hitting people and being physical and aggressive. It can take a lot of reps and a lot of months, but they will come around. It's a growth process.

We had a 5'10", 175-pound offensive tackle a couple years ago named Spencer Chahin who played on the scout team. He was tough. He was a guy who could hit. He got whipped most of the time, but he had his victories, too, and his biggest victory was that he endured all that and was never hurt and never gave up. It was beautiful. Chahin was very valuable, and I respected him as much if not more than any of our starters and I recognized him at our banquet. Pound for pound he was the toughest kid on our team. That kid walked away from our program with his head held high feeling good about himself, too.

The only way kids are going to learn to strike, block, tackle, and be physical is on the practice field. Teaching a team to be physical and play the game with the level of aggression it takes to be successful while at the same time preventing injuries is as difficult as anything a coach must do.

When we do team work, it's live, 100 percent, and full speed. Nobody tackles the quarterback, and we don't take anybody to the ground, but our team work is live and full go. This philosophy can bite you. We admit it. If you are as physical as we are in practice, especially if you have big kids and therefore a lot of major collisions, you're asking for trouble. But if your team is not hitting, you have to teach them how to hit. There are risks to that. You're opening yourself up to injury, but you have to in order to become successful.

Two-a-days are now illegal in California, and they should be. We put so much time into our summer program that I never felt like we needed two practices. The second practice was usually a waste of time because everybody is so sore and beat up anyway. Two-a-days are archaic, if you ask us, especially when we're trying to protect kids from concussions more than ever.

Starting this year, the California Interscholastic Federation rules prevent teams from having more than two 90-minute padded practices per week, and, even though we believe the only place you can learn to hit and physically move people is on the practice field, that's all you need at this level. If we feel our players haven't learned to play with the aggression and physicality we require, we do more sled work. That's not a full-contact drill, and virtually our whole team can use their sled to work on striking, blocking, and shedding techniques.

Sometimes a coach can be oblivious because he gets caught up trying to improve his team. A couple seasons ago, it was late in the year, and Coach Eidson started counting the offensive plays we ran in practice. Late in the week, he wrote "85" on the chalkboard and circled it. That's how many plays we had run.

We have been in the state title game since the current state playoff format began in 2006. The state championship game is typically our 15th game of the season. If we would run 100 plays a week, we wouldn't have a team left by Week 15.

||||||||||||||||||||||||||||||||||||||||||||||||||||||||||||||||||||||||||||

Typical Week

By former De La Salle head coach Bob Ladouceur and De La Salle quarterbacks coach Mark Panella

Here's a typical week for us during the season.

MONDAY is an offensive day. A lot of our kids play both ways. Two-way players report to their offensive coach on offensive day and to their defensive coach on defensive day. Players who don't have an offensive position report to their defensive position coach for individual and group technique work and often help out by being bag men or holding the bags and pads we use to represent where the opponents will line up during group and team work.

The offensive linemen will do their sled work for 20 minutes, and then we might set up the opposition's defensive line so they can see how they line up, how we're going to block them, or changes we might want to make in our blocking schemes. We might even install or reintroduce a play or two that we think will work against that week's opponent.

Meanwhile, quarterbacks and running backs work on ballhandling drills before we use bag men to replicate the opposition's defense while we discuss adjustments we might want to make against a particular defense or install a play or two to run against that week's opponent. Receivers and defensive backs might work on press coverage techniques for the first 20 minutes before the skill position players come together with the linebackers and safeties for a seven-on-seven session against a scout team that has already studied film of our upcoming opponent and therefore knows the schemes and individual player techniques they will be replicating.

Then we all come together for team work, during which time we also work on the punt and PAT/field goal teams. If we're working on offense, Terry may call out "punt team," and they have to scramble onto the field like they would in a game.

In recent years, we've taken the last 15 minutes of an offensive day to introduce defensive concepts we will install in much greater detail the following afternoon. We usually run 15 scout-team plays against our first-team defense. On defensive days we flip it and run 15 offensive plays at the end of practice. On Mondays we end practice with 35 minutes in the weight room.

TUESDAY is essentially like Monday with a defensive emphasis. Tuesday is another day where we put heavy emphasis on one on ones. We also work on the punt return and kickoff return teams. We end the on-field session with heavy conditioning, which means gassers.

WEDNESDAY is a combination day. We typically do 20 minutes of group offensive work, 20 minutes of group defensive work, a half hour of offensive team work, and a half hour of defensive team work. We also work approximately 15 live special teams plays into our normal workout. Kick return is the big emphasis on Wednesday, but we will also work on field goal, punt, and quarterback punt. Wednesday's practice also includes position-specific conditioning. Lineman will do rapid progression sled work; running backs and quarterbacks will pull tires; receivers and defensive backs will run and cover seem routes, bombs, deep outs, etc. in rapid progression.

THURSDAY is a later practice start because we have our prayer service in the chapel immediately after school. We don't wear pads. Most programs would call our Thursday practices a "walk-through," but we don't walk. We call ours "run-throughs."

We start practice with special teams. That's the day we work with our kickoff, kickoff return, and field goal/PAT teams. Coach Eidson works on onside kicks and special teams trick plays, after which we will put our offense on the field against a scout team of bag men, and we'll run an up-tempo series down the field with the first team. Then we will turn around and do a similar fast-paced offensive series with the second team before we roll the first team down the field again using plays that we expect to run in a similar sequence in the game the following evening. We finish the offensive portion of practice with a last series of first and second-teamers mixed together before we do the exact same thing with our first and second-team defense using an offense of scout-team players and bag men. We usually spend approximately a half hour on all three phases and we break early so the kids can get showered and commute to the site of our traditional Thursday night team meeting.

Scouting an Opponent
By former De La Salle head coach Bob Ladouceur

I always tried to study at least two of the opponents' games from the current season, and if we played them the year before, I would look at that to see how they tried to defend us and identify plays they ran offensively that we had trouble stopping. Sunday always involved a heavy workload for at least one coach, and for 34 years, that was me. I charted the opponent's offense. That's how I helped the defense. I would chart every offensive play they ran and would use those charts to educate our scout team for the coming week of preparation.

It typically took me four hours to chart two games, and then I would start looking at the opponents' defense. Sundays were a 10-hour day for me. For assistant coaches, who were also watching film, it was a three or four-hour day. I would divide a legal-sized piece of paper into four frames with five linemen already embossed in the frame. At the top was space for down and distance, hash mark, and yard line. I might write: left hash, first and 10, and then the play. I would draw our base defense against their offensive formation and would note how I would assume they would block our defense based on how they were blocking the defense in the game I was watching. That way when I gave the plays to the scout team, they weren't trying to figure out who to block.

You would be surprised how many coaches can't chart games or struggle to do it. There's a lot of information that has to be absorbed, processed, and put to paper. I always included the depth of running backs. You have to chart tendencies with formations. How many times do they pass out of a certain formation, how many times do they run, where do they run, where do they pass? I would draw lines from the receiver who caught the ball to better gauge the depth of the route. If you just draw a curl pattern on a piece of paper, the kids don't know if it's an eight-yard curl or a 16-yard curl. I would chart their alignment because sometimes a receiver lines up inside and runs an out and sometimes he lines up outside and runs an in. What formations do they like to pass out of and what formations do they use when they run? Where do they pass and where do they run out of those formations? You have to study the personnel groupings and what plays they like to run when certain combinations of players are on the field.

There's a lot of minutia in scouting. I always had to look at a play at least five times to get all their blocking assignments down, all the routes down, all the backfield motion, the depth of the running backs. You get a lot of tells that way. That all has to be noted on the scout sheet.

I would chart an opponent's three games play by play from start to finish and then I would have the scout team run those same plays in the same order against our starting defense during practice that week. Teams stick pretty close to what they've done in the past. They usually stay true to their tendencies. I know we do. We'd usually get through at least two full games of plays with the scout team so the defense saw the equivalent of two full games run against them. Running an opponent's plays in a specific order based on film study gives defensive players a feel for what the opponent was going to do early in the game, late in the game, in short yardage, long yardage, goal line, etc. We did it that way for my entire career.

Another useful tool is to go back and look at your previous game against the same opponent. You always think they are going to change something or do something different. That's always a possibility, and sometimes they did, but for the most part, teams do what they did the year before with only a slight variation. They might tweak it or blitz more or call plays differently, but it's too difficult to change what you've installed as your base offense or defense for one opponent.

If it's a team we haven't played, I have to guess how they would block our defense or block our front as if I were the opponent. Sometimes you can find a team that runs similar offense to what we run, but that's never easy because there are so few two-back offenses these days. We can watch tons of film of an upcoming opponent and never see them play a two-back set, which makes it hard to figure out what they'll run against us. What we usually see is defenses put another man in the box. Sometimes they will replace a defensive back with a linebacker. That's okay. We can block another defender in the box. We can still get by. If they put two in the box, it becomes a problem. We have to work our play-action pass and try to get outside. It's tougher to stuff the ball down their throats.

We study their personnel, who may be tough to block, and who we may want to attack more, but we really don't shy away from good players. We take that as a challenge to our linemen, and more often than not, our guys rise to the occasion. They like to go against a tough opponent. You always look at their dangerous guys, the ones who can really hurt you. You've got to stop what they do best and their best players. I'm also looking for space and big plays when I'm scouting an opponent. I'm trying to fool some of their players and get a big play behind them. That's what we'll practice during the week. We're definitely looking for areas we can exploit.

We never met as a staff on Sundays, but we were on the phone to each other all day trading tidbits. We should do this. Did you see that? Even though I charted the opposing offense, Coach Eidson was awesome at watching personnel and finding tendencies. When I came in on

Monday, he already knew what he wanted to run and why. I might say, "Look out for this," or "This is a strong tendency," but he already knew. I never charted the opposing offense for him or any of his assistants because they saw the same things I saw. My charts were for the kids. I would usually ask Coach Panella and Coach Alumbaugh to come in Monday with four or five plays they like. They were usually the same

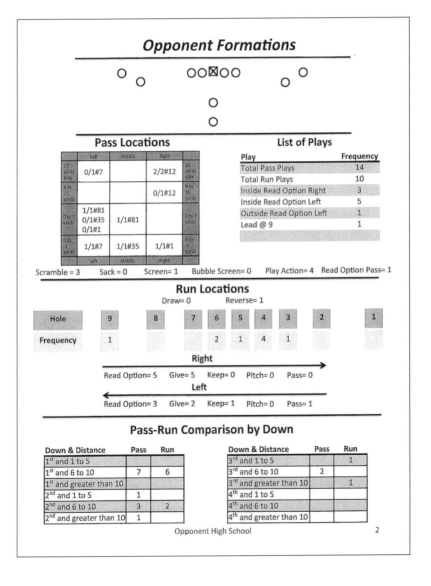

Opponent Formations

Pass Locations

	Left	Middle	Right	
15 yards plus	0/1#7		2/2#12	15 yards plus
8 to 15 yards			0/1#12	8 to 15 yards
0 to 7 yards	1/1#81 0/1#35 0/1#1	1/1#81		0 to 7 yards
0 to -5 yards	1/1#7	1/1#35	1/1#1	0 to -5 yards
	Left	Middle	Right	

List of Plays

Play	Frequency
Total Pass Plays	14
Total Run Plays	10
Inside Read Option Right	3
Inside Read Option Left	5
Outside Read Option Left	1
Lead @ 9	1

Scramble = 3   Sack = 0   Screen= 1   Bubble Screen= 0   Play Action= 4   Read Option Pass= 1

Run Locations

Draw= 0   Reverse= 1

Hole	9	8	7	6	5	4	3	2	1
Frequency	1			2	1	4	1		

Right →

Read Option= 5   Give= 5   Keep= 0   Pitch= 0   Pass= 0

← **Left**

Read Option= 3   Give= 2   Keep= 1   Pitch= 0   Pass= 1

Pass-Run Comparison by Down

Down & Distance	Pass	Run	Down & Distance	Pass	Run
1st and 1 to 5			3rd and 1 to 5		1
1st and 6 to 10	7	6	3rd and 6 to 10	2	
1st and greater than 10			3rd and greater than 10		1
2nd and 1 to 5	1		4th and 1 to 5		
2nd and 6 to 10	3	2	4th and 6 to 10		
2nd and greater than 10	1		4th and greater than 10		

Opponent High School

2

plays I'd been thinking about. We don't meet as a staff until right before Monday's practice, but we saw the same things and were on the same page.

‖‖

Video

By De La Salle video coordinator Tony DeMattei

Video has always been a hobby of mine. When my son played at De La Salle several years ago, I would videotape his games. Coach Eidson noticed what I was doing and asked if I could help the team with a digital video system they were trying to implement. When I started doing it, they were having trouble transitioning from VHS to digital and they didn't really have anybody who understood how it all worked. They had purchased a software program that was supposed to combine video from two cameras, but they were having trouble putting the end zone shots and sideline shots together. They weren't using the tools to the best of their ability. Because I understood how digital video worked, I was able to record in such a way that the sideline film and end zone film used the software to its full capability.

After watching several film sessions with the team and learning how much the coaches focused on technique, it dawned on me that it would be important to video practices because it would give kids more immediate feedback than just filming the games. A few years ago, I started filming not just the team work but the drills because the footwork is so important, and it has changed the program a little bit.

They used to review game video and watch the kids' techniques on Saturday. The rest of the week they would study scout video of the opposing team, but now they rely on the kids watching scout video online and they watch more practice video during the week so they can immediately correct mistakes.

One thing we do that might be different from most programs is we come up with different angles. I use four cameras, two on the sideline and two in the end zone with one camera from each location set to wide angle and tight angle. Coach Eidson can see the defensive backfield and receivers running their routes. Coach Lad and Coach Alumbaugh like the tight angles so they can see what the linemen are doing much more clearly. I even fooled around and connected the cameras to a remote control so I can mount them higher, even in the press box, and run two cameras simultaneously to get better shots. To be honest I don't know if the extra angles are necessary, but they are helpful when focusing on the linemen's footwork.

We lost the 2013 state championship game, and everybody was frustrated afterward because they were having trouble verbally communicating what was happening on the field. That same year the National High School Football Association changed its rule to allow any form of media on the sideline, so we cobbled together a system that allows us to watch video on the sideline during games.

Through trial and error, we developed a server and broadcast network that allows us to broadcast over two-and-a-half miles. It has been a huge bonus for us. We can pull images directly from our cameras on a few seconds delay and show them to kids on the sideline using iPads. The kids come off the field much more educated about what happened. Another benefit is we don't have to spend as much time watching film because we saw a lot of it on the field during the game.

People always ask us how we can afford such a system, but we can put one together with one used laptop, an app that costs less than $2, and an iPad. We have helped several other schools install similar systems. We run a cable to our camera to a digital encoder that digitizes video and saves it to a file. Another piece of software transmits the video to the sideline where coaches access it with their iPads. The whole process takes 15 to 30 seconds and has worked out very well for us.

Film Study

By former De La Salle head coach Bob Ladouceur

I never really thought about it until I started working on this book, but the fact that all of the students at our school have lunch at the same time is a big advantage for us because during the season we use that time to watch film with the kids. We have a 40-minute lunch break so the kids have 10 minutes to grab something to eat while watching films. A lot of the kids bring sack lunches. I met with offensive players in the weight room (Coach Alumbaugh meets with them now), and Coach Eidson meets with defensive players in his classroom. On Monday we usually introduce the opposing team's offense and defense so the kids can get a first taste of what they will see from the scout team in practice.

We try to make the films interactive. We want players to recognize formations and then call out plays they like to run out of the formation. Since we started filming our practices, we find ourselves spending less time watching opponents' film with the kids because we can assemble cut-ups on the video hosting service Hudl, and the kids can watch that on their own. We have spent more time in recent years watching our practice film with the kids to correct mistakes we see and to emphasize coaching points we noticed while watching film of one on ones.

We still correct things in real time, but when they see it on film, it validates what we're seeing. If you keep telling a kid his first step is flat, he's going to roll his eyes and think, *Whatever.* When you give him actual visual proof, it reaffirms what you've been telling him. Instead of "whatever," he says, "Yes, Coach. I've got it." They understand it and know you're not just nagging or picking on them.

Hudl has helped us tremendously. It allows us to watch film much more efficiently. We can swap video with coaches online and have access to that film immediately. We can post clips and cut-ups of ourselves or our opponent that players can access from home or even on the bus on the way to a game. We can also monitor how much time individual players are spending logged into the site so we know who is studying and who isn't.

⁣‌‌⁣⁣

Scouting Reports

By De La Salle scouting coordinator and scout team coach Chris Crespi

Because the game has changed and everybody is running the spread offense, scouting has changed. No longer is the play set when the team comes to the line of scrimmage. Now a quarterback has three options. It's not just about scouting coaching tendencies anymore. Spread quarterbacks are making so many decisions on the field you have to study their tendencies, too.

If you don't study a bunch of games and statistically work out what the kids like to do and what they're comfortable doing, you're at a serious disadvantage. High school kids don't like to leave their comfort zone. For example, we discovered a few years ago that 87 percent of the time an opposing quarterback went to his left he kept the ball and ran. Because we knew that, our defense swallowed him up. You may discover that when inside the 40-yard line a quarterback will throw a post to his favorite receiver 80 percent of the time.

Defensive scouting hasn't progressed as much because there aren't as many decisions being made on the field. I produce two scouting reports every week—one for the coaches and a scaled down version for the players. If I gave the kids the same scouting report I gave the coaches, they would look at me like I had three heads. These kids are studying calculus, history, physics, and numerous other subjects so I try to keep my scouting reports of analysis with diagrammed plans attached to two pages or fewer. You have to be careful that you don't overload them. They don't want to let you down. They know how hard you're working for them and they don't want to disappoint you.

The trick is creating scouting reports that don't just get thrown into a backpack and never looked at again. I try to use phrases that will capture the kids' attention. I might say a running back can turn five into 10, and 10 into a touchdown because I hope it will help them remember that he is a dangerous player.

The second thing I focus on is artwork. These kids are used to playing *Madden* football and other video games with high-quality graphics, and if you give them hand-drawn X's and O's, they look right past it. I put a lot of effort into the artwork for my scouting reports, and the kids have responded well. I've now got a graphics library of more than 5,000 plays that I can alter depending on formations. Coaches these days put kids in a lot of different formations. I don't know if it's an ego thing, but it's confusing. You have to spend a lot of time teaching kids formations. We had a team that ran 52 different formations, but those kids didn't know what they were doing. Although it takes longer to gather data when scouting those teams, they are easy to decipher. Teams that run limited formations and concentrate on technique and execution are more difficult to scout. Which is easier, stopping a team that runs the same play out of 10 formations or the team that runs a play flawlessly and at breakneck speed out of one or two formations?

The key is identifying the metrics you want and ones you don't. A tendency is only valuable if it can be used. I look for a way to encode what happens after the ball is snapped. I've written some software, which helps. I chart the down and distance, field position, formation, personnel groups, and who touches the ball on a single line of data. I have a grid that charts where the quarterback throws on various downs. What hole does the running back run through? It's not as simple as 24 (two back through the four hole) dive anymore. Now the running back decides where to go. He gets to choose. Kids like to do what they're good at. I study what hole the guy likes to run through in certain situations and compare it to what holes the quarterback likes to run through. Who does the quarterback like to throw to? Is one guard less effective when pulling? People make choices, and those are the metrics I look for. You have to study those tendencies because they're different for every opponent.

I start on Friday night when I contact the opposing coach via Hudl and ask for his last three games. Coaches are very good about this. We usually get the film on Friday night, and I start looking at it without looking for anything in particular just to get a feel for what they like to do. On Saturday morning I start charting each play on a piece of paper and then I translate that play, formation, down and distance, and result into software code. Then I run a statistical analysis to spot trends. Are they passing the ball out of a certain formation or on a certain side of the field? Does the quarterback always keep the ball on third down because he wants to make something happen? Maybe we can go after him on third down because he always wants to do it himself. I'll pick the top 10 trends and put them into a report for coaches and maybe some players. I organize all the plays from all three games and laminate them for the scout team. I then condense those plays into a two-page summary that describes what that week's opponent likes to do when they run and pass. I might add some stats if I think it's meaningful. I will even describe why their best players are so effective if I feel that's important.

In the end, however, my job is to provide the coaching staff with the information they think is important rather than what I think is important. Regardless of what I come up with, if it doesn't help them, it's worthless. For example, every week I ask Coach Alumbaugh and Coach Eidson if there are any specific things they would like to see on the scouting report. Then before every practice, I send them a script of plays I plan to have the scout team run. They offer feedback if they want to see something specific. We usually stick to the script during practice but will occasionally make some real-time changes as needed. This process makes team work much more efficient.

Opponent High School Pass Notes

- **A Tale of Two Quarterbacks**

  The starting quarterback for Opponent was injured in the last game at the end of the first half. A wide receiver took his place. The first-team quarterback was the heart of the offense, and the coaches had even modified their offense to take advantage of his running and athletic skills. The replacement is an athlete as well, starting at wide receiver, but it is obvious that he has not had many reps at quarterback. He is still dangerous as he rallied the team in their last drive against another team to score the winning touchdown. The key play in this drive was a 30+ yard pass by the replacement. It is likely that the replacement will quarterback this week with plenty of reps behind him. Regardless of who is at quarterback, there are some common traits that the Opponent offense demonstrates.

- **2nd and Short, Go Long**

  When Opponent achieves good first down yardage that leaves them with less than 3 yards to go for a first down, they like to take a chance and throw deep.

- **Don't Let Them Have the Post**

  This phrase still rings in my ears from my college defensive coordinator, and it certainly applies to Opponent. For the games that we scouted, when Opponent threw for greater than 15 yards, greater than 90% of the time they threw to the middle of the field. That is sector 8 in our Pass-Tracking Map. They did complete one long pass to the right when they tried it once.

- **Protect the Passer**

  When not in Trips or Quads, Opponent most often puts two receivers into routes in any play and rarely puts more than 3. Either the tight end and/or the wing will stay in to protect the quarterback along with the running back. This gives the quarterback considerable time to wait until a receiver becomes open. When the defense falls asleep, they do like to sneak out the tight end and/or the running back into the pattern. In Trips and Quads, they will put the 4 receivers into the pattern.

- **Screens and Draws, Be Aware**

  Opponent will run traditional screens and draws when they have over 10 yards to get a first down. They also run a QB draw, with a twist at times, with an empty backfield. The twist is that the QB will not drop back and set up to pass before taking off up the middle. Instead, he will quickly shoot off the middle following the fold block by a guard and the center.

- **Not Many Bubbles**

  The bubble screen is in Opponent's portfolio, but they have not used it much. If they go to an inexperienced quarterback, they may have to use this more.

Opponent High School Run Notes

- **Disciplined Read Option Blocking with a Twist**

  Opponent exhibits very disciplined blocking assignments when running the inside and outside read options. They will not touch the End that the quarterback is going to read. For inside read options, they read the same man that previous teams read when they ran it. For the outside read option and fly sweep option, they change it up from other teams that they have faced. Instead of reading the end on the side from which the running back or receiver starts, they read the opposite side.

- **Collapse and Two is Better Than One**

  The read option at Opponent is based upon the traditional zone or read, rip, and run that we have seen previously. They function because of two blocks. First, on the option side where the end is left untouched, the outside blocker's first responsibility is to collapse his inside man down into the line. They are not just trying to get in the way, they are trying to push that inside man into the center of the line and cut off the linebacker's fill. At the same time, the onside guard is trying to cross the tackles face and get to the inside linebacker if possible.   Second, on the back side, they will often double team the tackle which again is designed to cut off the linebacker's fill and creates a wide path for the running back to run through on the backside. This is why, more often than not, when the QB gives on a read option the RB cuts back to the other side of the center. **There is a detailed description of Oppoenet's blocking strategy for the read option in the play packet. Both Defense and Scout Offense should read and understand it!!!**

- **Give or Keep**

  Prior to the starting quarterback's injury, this was a no brainer. He kept the ball nearly 50% of the time to both sides, which is a very high number than we have seen in previous games. With this new quarterback, he is more likely to give more than his predecessor, but that does not mean he is shy. He had some very good runs when he kept the ball in this last game.

- **If it Works, Don't Fix It**

  If a play works, Opponent will run it many times until they no longer have success. That goes for plays throughout the game as well as running the same play one right after the other.

- **Follow the Wing**

  When the wing is in the game, he will lead you to the play.

Plays
Anatomy of Read Option Blocking: Strongside

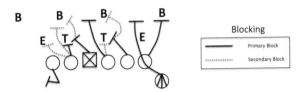

Above is the blocking scheme for a read option to the right, to the strong side. The blocking is a little different from the Rip, Reach, and Run that you have seen so far this year. Primary blocks are shown in black and secondary blocks are shown in orange. On the side of the read option, Opponent is very disciplined at leaving the Defensive End alone for the read. The play side tackle's primary responsibility is to collapse the tackle into the line. He does not move on to the linebacker until that Defensive Tackle has completely disappeared. The play side Guard's first move is to cross in front of the Defensive Tackle's face and get to the Linebackers. If he can not, he ends up double teaming the Defensive Tackle. The Center hits the back side DT until he disappears and then moves on to the backers. The back side guard's responsibility is to hit the DT first. If he is not there, he looks for the backer and then the backside DE. He then checks for the DE coming inside. The end result is usually a double team on the Backside DT with the center then slipping off to the linebacker. Rarely, the backside guard ends up double teaming the DE going to the B Gap, but it does happen. This is how Opponent sets up the running back cutting back to the backside on the give, and the quarterback keeping to the outside.

Plays
Inside Read Option Right ARC

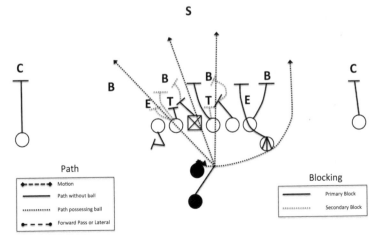

In addition to scouting your opponents, another way to help the coaching staff is to scout your own team. At certain points during the season, I attempt to identify tendencies by our offense and defense and give those results to our coaches, which makes us less predictable and forces opposing coaching staffs to spend more time preparing for us during the week because our tendencies are always evolving.

|||||||||||||||||||||||||||||||||||||||||||||||||||||||||||||||||||||||||||||||||||||||||||||||||||||||||

Scout Team

By De La Salle scouting coordinator and scout team coach Chris Crespi

As the scouting coordinator and coach of the scout team, I've got the most difficult coaching job in California because I have to play against De La Salle's starting offense and defense every day in practice. The kids on my scout team may not play as much on gameday as they would like to, but we coach them as hard as we do our starters and make sure they understand that they play a critical role in our preparation every week. If you're one of those coaches who just holds up a card and says, "Run this play" to your scout team, you're missing out on a lot of quality coaching opportunities. Some of our favorite success stories and most rewarding moments as coaches involve scout-team members. Our scout team guys take pride in what they're doing, and we take pride in coaching them.

By creating a unique team within the team, you not only give your starters a realistic look at what they can expect on gameday, but you engage second and third-string players who often feel disenchanted. Our scout team guys don't think of themselves as cannon fodder or meat bags. They're going out there to play fast and tough and make plays and hits. Our Most Valuable Scout Team Player is a prestigious reward. It means you're engaged, a team player, and helping the team prepare and win. We want our offense to face a scout team more difficult than the team they will play on Friday night, even if it's only in effort and technique. Practices become like games to them. They go crazy when they score a touchdown or stop our offense, and it's invaluable because it brings intensity to practices.

If the scout team does not perform during the week, the starters have a very difficult time on Friday night. We want our scout team to emulate the opponent's personnel and schemes as closely as possible. In recent years our scout team has risen to the challenge and has had a blast doing it. Because we use Hudl, the players have access to the same film as the coaches, allowing them to study the upcoming opponent on their own.

It's amazing how the kids have reacted. If you're a second or third-string defensive back or linebacker on our scout team, you not only need to know our assignments, but you need to know those of the opposing players who you will be imitating during practice during that week. Our players learn how our opponents line up and what their tendencies and responsibilities are. By Monday they've already started that process. Then they start decorating their uniforms to look like the opposing team and the opposing player they will be mimicking that week.

By Wednesday those guys know all the opposition's plays by heart. I can tell them to get in a quad formation and give me a read-option left, and they execute opposing schemes with speed and precision. We still have to constantly be on them because they lapse back into how we want them to play and not how the opponent plays, but that's human nature.

I have a line I like to use with the kids: "You pay for the education, but the culture is free." I mention this because Monday is also the day I introduce the country, culture, or part of the world the scout team will be learning about that week. It's fun to introduce more than football into these kids' lives. We were looking for something new to do when Lad suggested we have Polynesian week to celebrate heritage of the Pacific Islanders on the team because I lived in Hawaii for several years. We talked about Kamehameha and how he unified the islands. We wore leis. It was amazing to hear these kids sincerely and passionately debate whether the Bayonet Constitution and the subsequent annexation of the Islands were ethical. They were captivated the entire week. I called the team together with a conch shell. The kids loved it. All the players grew up watching *SpongeBob SquarePants*, and there's a memorable episode with a magic conch shell. The kids liked the conch shell so much that I still use it to call the scout team together, and our Scout Team Player of the Year receives an engraved conch shell at the postseason banquet.

It worked out so well that the next week we did Spain, then Mexico, then the Ivory Coast. We've studied France, the Netherlands, Taiwan, the People's Republic of China, among others.

We learn about the history and then we use words from that language when we make our calls at the line of scrimmage or to change plays during the week. When we were studying the Netherlands, any call to the left was "Dank je wel" or "thank you" in Dutch. Then each day we talk about historical events that happened in that country or culture while the kids stretch. The kids like it because it's something different. Sometimes there are almost fistfights about what country we're going to focus on during the upcoming week, but it keeps the kids engaged.

As the scout team coach, I watch film of every practice to find something we can run against the starters to fool them. I gameplan against them every day using the opposing team's plays. If the starting ends are crashing in, I might decide to do more rollouts, for example. Our goal is to make practice stop and make them find a solution to what we're doing.

We've had kids who have come up to us and said they want to play every scout-team snap for the rest of the season. They ask us to please not take them out. If we feel a kid can handle that commitment, if he's strong enough and tough enough, we let him do it. Attitudes like that make our starters appreciate and respect our scout team members.

I remember one of our scout team kids stood up in a team meeting before the state championship game last year and said, "We've taken you as a far as we can go. You have to take it the rest of the way." You could have heard a pin drop in the silence that ensued. The starters understood that they indeed owed a debt of gratitude to the scout team.

Gameplanning: Offense
By former De La Salle head coach Bob Ladouceur

From Sunday through Thursday, you're taking a crash course on your upcoming opponent. It's tough. You're concentrating week to week. All you have is that opponent. Everything else down the road doesn't matter. As soon as the game is over on Friday, another crash course begins. Sometimes when we're in the playoffs, we'll face an opponent we played earlier in the season, and I will have totally forgotten what they ran. You erase everything from your memory every week, and then all those teams start bleeding into one. The focus is intense. I have to watch film to remind myself of what happened two weeks before.

But when I meet with the team at lunch time on Monday, I have to have a plan so I can start feeding them information. Sometimes I would only have half a gameplan on Monday. I've put in wrinkles as late as Thursday that we've used successfully in a game. You always have to be accessing what you're doing. We never ran plays in a game that we didn't execute well in practice.

Too many coaches try to outsmart the competition and end up outsmarting themselves. That's the biggest mistake that I consistently see coaches make, and we've been guilty of it at times ourselves. Every coach wants to do his part. He wants to make an impact, be the difference. Egos can even become involved depending on who's on the other sideline.

We keep our offense consistent. We'll throw a wrinkle play in here or there. We'll throw a couple plays in per week if we think we can get a quick score because of what we see as a weakness. Maybe we feel we can get behind their secondary or we adjust a pattern to exploit something we see. But they're usually plays that were already in our playbook. I never come in and say, "We've got to run these five new plays." Then you end up spending your entire week installing plays they haven't run

Coaching high school football is very time-consuming. As part of my exhaustive preparation, I come up with 10 run plays and 15 pass plays for the upcoming game. (Photo by Bob Larson)

yet or formations they haven't seen. It's too time-consuming, especially when you have as many two-way players as we do.

I don't think about what we're going to put in this week to fool the opposing team. We have enough plays to beat them. What I worry about is, *Are these guys drilled well enough, disciplined enough, and tough enough to beat them?* Those are the questions that most frequently determine success. I'll come out Monday sometimes before I've had a lot of time to watch game film and see a lot of our opponent's defense and what was successful against it and I'll see a few running plays and a few passing plays that I want to work on that day. That's an intensive day for me. Because Tuesday is a defensive day, I don't have to have anything solid until Wednesday afternoon.

Ideas come to me at different times. I could be driving home after practice and I'll go, *I've got to run that play. That will work.* Or I will be sitting in class, and it will come to me. Or I'll be lying in bed and I will think, *I like that play.* It eventually comes to me.

I attended a workshop about how people learn several years ago. Some guys know right away. They'll see a problem and then see a solution. Another guy has to see it and think about it. They call them percolators. That's how I came up with gameplans. I can't do it in one sitting. I can't do it on Sunday night. I've got to think about it for a while. I've got to play it out in my head.

To give the kids a sense of confidence offensively, I come up with 10 run plays and 15 pass plays that I would like to run against the upcoming opponent and I narrow it down from there. I also like to tell them when I expect to run a particular play. I might tell them the first plays to start the game will be these two runs and this pass, or that we might run that screen pass if we're on the hash mark, and it's third and long. That way, they know what to expect and are better prepared.

||||||||||||||||||||||||||||||||||||||||||||||||||||||||||||||||||||||||||||||||||||||||||

Gameplanning: Defense

By De La Salle defensive and special teams coordinator Terry Eidson

I spent a lot of time preparing for our game against Southern California power Mater Dei High in 1998. It was the first time a Northern California team had played a powerhouse from Southern California. It was a huge game, and I broke down their offense and decided that I was going to make all these defensive adjustments based on their formations. On the first day of practice, the kids were running around like chickens with their heads cut off. After a half hour of pure frustration, I went back and said, "Let's do what we do and do it well." Anytime you try to adjust on the fly, it just doesn't work with high school kids.

We might start studying a team over the summer and think about how we would like to run a specific line stunt against them, but then we can't get the first step down. Everybody wants to outscheme everybody, but the first thing you have to do is get your defense to play your defense from the basics on down. If we can't even do that, why would we do something new? Every year I try to put in something new and then I can't get the basic stuff installed and I think, *What's the point?*

It's not about schemes. You have to get your guys to be technically sound so they know what they're doing. If they don't know what they're doing, they're going to get their butts kicked. It's that simple. We go with what we have and we live with it. Sometimes we'll work on something all week and then dump it on Thursday because we're not executing it properly. All you need are a few basic rules you live or die with and learn to play those rules consistently.

Playcalling

By former De La Salle head coach Bob Ladouceur

A lot of the coaching on gameday is in the moment. In the pros they take all the emotion out of it. They decide what plays they are going to run from the 40-yard line to the 40-yard line, so they take all the thinking out of it and do all the preparation ahead of time.

Personally, I don't like that. I always thought of playcalling as something you have to feel as you go along. I've always had a feel for seeing 11 people out there on defense and knowing where they're short, where they're vulnerable. If I see that they are short in a particular area or if their defense is weak somewhere, I attack. I'll see that their corners are playing our receivers two yards inside, so I'll run out routes or I'll run guys down the sidelines. If they're playing two yards outside, I will run inside routes.

I can look at their secondary to see if they are peeking into the backfield. Sometimes I'll run a play, and the secondary will take one step back and then come off the receiver for run support. Then I know it's time to call a play-action pass and I know our guy will be wide open. If I come into a situation and have a different play on, I might look at their defense and say, "If I'm in this situation again, third and long, and we're on the hash, I'll run the screen back to the other side." I'll kind of catalogue it in my head and I'll talk to the players. When they come to the sideline, I'll tell them that we're going to run the screen next time on third and long, and they'll start nodding their heads, and you can see they're excited about it and that their confidence is growing.

I relied on Coach Alumbaugh a lot when calling plays. He would watch the down lineman and the linebackers. Coach Panella would watch the corners and tell me how they were playing us. During a series they are answering my questions. Are they playing deep? Squatting? Lining up inside or outside? What play do you like? They always had a suggestion.

If a play doesn't work, they will come to me and say, "Don't worry. This guy missed a block or went the wrong way. It will work." You have to have a feel for playcalling, and they both have a good feel for it, too.

If they want to do anything besides answer my questions, the rule was always to let me know when I'm not calling plays. In between series we have an open dialogue, but when people interrupt me in the middle of a series, it's really distracting. I couldn't concentrate when people talked to me in the middle of a drive. I'd get stuck once in a while and would ask Coach Alumbaugh or Coach Panella for a play. I didn't run into that too much because—when I was calling a game—I always had something in the back of my mind for third and long. I would think to myself, *What can I get these guys with the next time we're in this situation?* If they were overplaying the strong side, maybe I would want to run something back to the weak side. I always had something in mind, and it would usually pop up again the next time I got in that situation. But if people are putting other plays in my head, I would have trouble retrieving it.

That's why I rarely wore headsets on the sideline. I could see the game fine and I didn't like other people in my ear. When I did wear a headset, it was just so the coaches could hear me call the play and send the right personnel into the game.

I always watched the opposing safeties as a play caller to see how they reacted to our runs. Safeties have a tendency to stare into the backfield and watch. I'd watch those guys to see what they are looking for. You could tell if they are looking at a receiver or into the backfield. When they were looking into the backfield, I knew I could burn those guys. That was always my philosophy.

I would always go into a game with a couple passing plays picked out that I thought would work. I would study film from the previous year and watch a team that did something similar to what I wanted to do and I would watch the secondary and how they react to runs. If you're running the football and they're getting nosy and creeping up, I try to burn those guys. I go for the home run and try to break their backs.

Our kids get excited about that. I might tell them, "We've only got one shot at this pass because we're not going to be able to beat them twice on the same thing." We'd practice it over and over, especially before a championship game. We would drill it and then find the time to run it, and it was almost always successful.

It's also important to listen to your players when you're calling plays or making adjustments. They often have better information on how the opposing team is playing than you do. Sometimes when something isn't working, the best thing you can do is ask them what they're seeing. We were preparing to play Long Beach Poly High in 2001 in one of the biggest games in school—maybe even state—history. They were so fast that I knew if we tried to outflank them they would beat us. We decided we were going to run up the gut as much as we could. We wanted to get upfield as quickly as possible by running right over center. We noticed on film that they left the middle open.

Our quarterback at the time was Matt Gutierrez, who would go on to play at Michigan, at Idaho State, and in the NFL. He started checking out of that run and running something different. I would tell him to run the darn play. He would say, "They're sitting in double ones." They had a gameplan, too, and they wanted to take away the run up middle. I couldn't see it from the sideline. He kept telling me that they were not running the defense we practiced against all week. I thought he was panicking. I told him to get out there and run it, but he kept checking out of it. He was adamant about it. Later, when I looked at the film, the kid was absolutely right. He'd been making great calls, and here I was hassling him the whole game.

» GAME MANAGEMENT

PREGAME Our philosophy has always been if they're not ready to play the night before the game at our Thursday night meeting, nothing anybody else says before Friday's game is going to change that. Nothing will make them play better. It's not going to happen. We never felt like it was my responsibility to fire kids up. We don't want assistant coaches to feel as if they have to get the kids ready to play and we don't want the kids feeling as if they have to get each other ready to play. That's all false emotion. It's meaningless. Motivation has to come from inside each individual player. We might say stuff occasionally if we feel we needed to, or if I felt I could sum up the gravity of the game in a few lines. Former player Steve Lilly shot film of me talking to the team before a championship game for a documentary about our program he was working on. I could tell that team was uptight and said: "I don't expect a perfect performance. But what I do expect—and what you should expect of yourselves and one another—is a perfect effort from snap to whistle." Lilly titled his documentary *Perfect Effort*. They used that line in the movie *When the Game Stands Tall*, and it has taken on a life of its own. More often, I would say something like: "Don't clip on the kickoff return."

SIDELINE RULES Coaches can get emotional. We always want to make sure everybody is calm and on an even keel. We, for example, never want coaches yelling at kids. If a coach gets after the officials, the kids will feed off it and will learn bad habits. Our rule was only the head coach or assistant coach Joey Aliotti could talk to the officials. Coach Aliotti knows all those guys on a first-name basis so it makes sense for him to be the go-between if we need an explanation. Coach Eidson always gets in his two cents, too, of course. He doesn't yell at them; he just annoys them. We're all watching our players, but Coach Aliotti watches to see whether the man was illegally downfield or if the quarterback crossed the line of scrimmage. He is also excellent with clock management so we rely on him for that, too.

Every coach has a role, and every coach must execute that role. One guy might be in charge of personnel groupings, another in charge of substitutions. For example, assistant special teams/secondary coach Boyce is in charge of special teams personnel because Coach Eidson is often talking to the defense and may not notice when the starting guard, who also happens to be the long snapper, is being evaluated by the medical staff.

Position coaches should coach their own kids and not another coach's position. Don't watch the game like a spectator. Watch your guys. Help your players and keep your emotions out of it or you'll fluster them.

As for the players themselves, the backups should be watching and supporting the starters, and when the starters come out, we don't want them screwing around. We want them supporting the backups the way the backups were supporting them. That really isn't a problem for us. We've found that our starters get more excited when our second and third-team guys make plays than when they're making plays themselves.

HALFTIME Every halftime has a different feel depending on what's happening in the game. In our opinion the idea of making dramatic halftime adjustments is a myth. Generally, it's a time to sit back, take a breath, and reassess. Where are they hurting us? Why are they hurting us? You have to decide to either continue down the current path or make changes to get on a better path. If you've found a scab or something that works, keep picking at it until it's gone.

For us the importance of halftime has been diminished because we now can review video on the sideline so we're examining what's working, what's not working, and why during the actual game. The one thing halftime does is give us a chance to review with the two-way players what we've already talked about with the one-way players on the sideline.

Offensively, we might show them how we're going to block a certain play because they were blocking it wrong or we might give them four or five plays that we want to run a lot in the second half so it's not a surprise. Defensively, we always want them to be confident. Coach Eidson might ask if there's something we're running that they don't like. What are we running that you guys feel is working? If we lacked focus or were unmotivated, we might get after them a little bit.

BLOWOUT Our average score during our 151-game winning streak was 44–10, and being on the other side of a beatdown is not fun. Nobody deserves to have their nose rubbed in it. These are kids. It's easy to get caught up with the guy on the other sideline, especially if there's a rivalry there. It's a competitive situation, but always remember you're dealing with kids. We're the adults. There's no excuse for demoralizing kids.

We have a lot of guys who work as hard as our starters. Whenever we feel a game is in hand, we start subbing immediately. A lot of guys have earned playing time and deserve to be in at the first opportunity they can. Generally, we consider the first half fair game. We don't really make wholesale changes in the first half unless it's blatantly out of hand. Everybody should be able to play a half of football. We have to play our guys. They have to get their reps. We want to keep our starters in the game during the first half. We'll normally start subbing out guys after the first series of the second half, but we still allow our second and third-stringers to throw the ball and run the offense. We're not throwing bombs or trying to score, but we'll throw a seven-yard pass on third and 6 even if the second or third-stringers are in there. They should have a chance to execute the offense. If you're second or third-string wide receiver and you've worked hard on the scout team, an eight-yard hitch isn't going to hurt anybody. That's fair game. They've earned that opportunity. There are also times when late in the game we slow our offense to a crawl and purposely run plays we don't think will work as effectively.

The last thing any coach wants to happen is to lose a starter during a lopsided game. We've done a good job of protecting our starters. We give our backups a chance. We could probably own a lot of individual state records if we cared about stats, but we're not going to leave somebody in a game to break a record.

POSTGAME For us the postgame locker room was never a place to celebrate a win. It was time for honest evaluation, looking at what we saw, what we did well, what we didn't do well. We don't hesitate to be critical and we don't hesitate to be complimentary. Because we typically have to look at film for details, the postgame evaluation relates more to the effort, heart, and intensity displayed because that can be evaluated more quickly.

CHAPTER 4

Offense

The goal is to impose our will.

—Former De La Salle head coach Bob Ladouceur

I installed the veer when I took over in 1979 because my top assistant at the time played in Bill Yeoman's offense at University of Houston and knew it inside and out. It appealed to me because it relied on quickness and precision more than size and athleticism, and we didn't have much size or athleticism in those days. I thought it could give average players the best chance to succeed.

It's an archaic offense now that everyone's running the spread, which is why I won't spend much time on it in this book. Virtually every year for the past three-plus decades, I've questioned the wisdom of keeping it as our base offense. I've had time to reflect since I stepped down from the head coaching job and I've realized that our outdated offense has been amazingly productive. Our team has averaged more than 40 points per game during my 34 years as head coach. We have scored 70 or more points five times, 60 or more on 41 occasions, and 50-plus in 115 games.

Maybe there's something to be said for the veer because we have been so productive using it. It helps that nobody else runs it. Teams can't simulate our get-off and precision in practice, and we are often able to jump to a big lead before the other team settles in, adjusts to our speed and quickness, and gets their feet under them.

In my opinion it doesn't matter what you run as long as your offense has the same mentality as your defense, which means it's aggressive and attacks. We try to get teams on their heels with an up-tempo style that prevents defenses from making adjustments at the line of scrimmage. The goal is to impose our will. We take what the defense gives us, but we also dictate what they can give us. Regardless of how exotic they want to be, they have to account for the dive back, the quarterback, and the pitch back. We welcome blitzes. That plays into our blocking schemes.

That's why I don't put as heavy an emphasis on the pass as the run because an offense is much more aggressive running the ball. Nothing is more demoralizing to a defense than when an offense is running the ball consistently, not just moving the chains and eating up the clock but being more aggressive and physical, which is why I believe the offense's premier unit is the offensive line.

Our offensive linemen always needed to be strong, fast, aggressive, and have great get-off. Those attributes were always more important to us than size. When you have a unit like that that works together and respects each other, you can put average runners behind it, and they will make substantial yardage. We've done that before many times.

The key to any offense is our offensive linemen giving our running backs an opportunity by winning the neutral zone. It's the No. 1 rule of football. The neutral zone is the most important part of the field. Own that one yard and you will be successfully attacking the defense. Whether you're watching film of an offense making yards on your defense or your offense making yards on an opposing defense, it's the same principle. It's about winning the line of scrimmage and battling people off the ball. You don't have to destroy people, but you have to make forward progress.

Nothing gives an offense more confidence than knowing it can get one yard in a tough situation. We train for that. We prepare our kids to push people off the ball on fourth and 1 or fourth and 2 to the extent that it almost becomes an afterthought. When we cross the 50-yard line, we go for it on fourth down virtually every time if it's reasonable. That's how confident we are that we can win the neutral zone, even though against many elite opponents through the years, we have been outweighed by 20, 30, 40, and even 50 pounds per man.

We can offset the opposition's size advantage with technique and fundamentals. We are a fundamental football team. Eighty percent of what we do is fundamental-oriented and/or drill work, and it's done in individual group periods. I'm not going to be scheme-specific in this section because it doesn't really matter what offense you run if you win the battle up-front. If we have a breakdown, if someone can't make a block, it goes back to steps, technique, body position, get-off. It's the same fundamental things every time.

Approximately 80 percent of the teams we've played in recent years have run the spread, and that's a conservative estimate. My only philosophical difference with the spread is that it's a passive offense that attempts to shield or wall off defenders so running backs have options when choosing holes. Those teams are easier to defend in my opinion. If you can keep their offensive linemen at the line of scrimmage and your linebackers fill their lanes, you can be solid against the run. It's when you're knocking guys off the ball, pushing them back, and turning them that you're creating creases and lanes in the defense—or at least that has been my experience.

The spread is trendy for a reason. It's a good offense. If you take it from a traditional sense of football, the quarterback is running the option. He's handing the ball off. When you have a running quarterback, you have 12 players. That's the philosophy behind it. You have another option out there. It gives you another receiver, and you still have two runners in the backfield. It puts pressure on your defense because when an offense spreads you out and has guys from sideline to sideline, you've got your whole secondary out there and it looks like grandpa's teeth because there's so much space in between. I understand the philosophy and why it's popular. We run some of it, too, and we've been successful running it, but we run it with an aggressive offensive line charge. We don't zone block it. We go after people.

What we've discovered in recent years is that because most of our opposing teams play against the spread in practice and in games that they have a hard time dealing with us coming straight off the ball and getting in their faces. We were preparing for a state championship game a few years ago against a team with two inside linebackers, Butch Pauu and Matthew Inman, who were Division I recruits. I watched a ton of film on those guys, and they were making tons of tackles at or behind the line of scrimmage. I saw teams run away from them and throw it over their heads. What I didn't see was an offense that attacked the second level and got in their grills.

We opened the game running right at those guys and scored on our first six possessions in what turned into a 48–8 win. Don't get me wrong. Those linebackers were great players, but they hadn't had to fight off blocks like that all season because they hadn't played against teams with aggressive offensive lines.

Because we've had so much success running the ball, our most effective passes are play-action passes. Even when we pass protect, it looks like we're run blocking. We fire out, pull, and back block, and the defensive line freezes, thinking run. It keeps the linebackers true to their responsibilities first, which is what we're looking for. We put a premium on carrying out the play-action passes with great fakes, and they are by far our most efficient pass plays. When we run our play-action plays, the goal is to break a guy wide open behind the entire secondary. Those are backbreakers.

When I call the plays, I watch the safeties. If you're running the football, a defense either moves them forward or plays them at eight yards. I'm always confident we can sneak a receiver behind them and kill them on huge plays. Our stats for passing always look something like 15 attempts and seven completions, but we'll have 180 yards or so because we gashed their secondary. If I was defending us, I would keep the safeties back, tell them to read their keys as best they can, but don't give up the 35-yard drag route.

Offensive Line

By former De La Salle head coach Bob Ladouceur and current De La Salle head coach Justin Alumbaugh

Our offense scored 63 points in the 2014 California Open Division State Championship Game. We had 595 total yards, 559 rushing yards, and nine rushing touchdowns in the game to cap the most prolific offensive season in school history. We had a school-record 5,660 rushing yards and a 53 points-per-game average. That season our starting running backs each had more than 1,800 rushing yards and averaged more than 10 yards per carry, prompting more emails from coaches asking the one question that has been asked of us more than any other.

How does your offensive line get off the ball so quickly?

The first thing to know is overweight kids can't move quickly and certainly not for the entire game. They will wear out. I don't mean to disparage anyone or any team. In some zone blocking schemes, bigger is better, but we have our own system and we train our offensive linemen to be lean. That means you have to build lean muscle during the offseason, and they must be in great shape.

We started measuring our players' body fat several years ago. In 2010 we had one of our best offensive lines, and the starting lineman with the highest percentage of body fat measured 12.6. Our heaviest lineman had the lowest percentage that year, a tick under 5 percent. We were a little heavier in 2014.

Our linemen are strong, but we also make them run 400s on the track. A couple years ago we had a 260-pound lineman who could run the 400 meters in 60 seconds. Even in the weight room, our kids are in constant motion, which keeps their heart rate up and burns fat.

Because our offensive linemen are in great condition and employ proper fundamentals, we can fire off the ball quickly. (Photo by Bob Larson)

You've got to decide what is important to you and your program. If you want to emphasize speed over size, the way we do it all starts with building lean muscle during the offseason.

Stance
We instruct right-footed players to line up with the toe of their right foot aligned with the ball of the left foot. We want no more than three to four inches between the tip of the right toe and the inseam of the left foot. The feet should be hip width apart. Kids often want their stance to be wider because they don't have flexibility in their hips, and it's easier to get down in their stances if their feet are wider. We use specific exercises (more on that later) to create flexibility in the hips and demand that our linemen's feet aren't more than an inch or two outside their shoulders.

It's all about balance. They must be able to move in either direction.

When they are preparing to get in a set position, we tell the right-handed player to reach with his right hand so he can just touch a blade of grass, then fall forward three inches forward into his stance. I want to see just a little bit of space between their left heel and the ground and I want to see an inch of space between their right heel and the ground. A lot of kids want to be on their toes. They want to lift their heels off the ground, but then they become heavy in their stances because there's too much weight on their hand and all they can do is lunge off the ball. That's not what we want. In order to have a strong base, the feet must be underneath the hips.

Once our linemen are in their stance, someone should be able to eat dinner off their back. Their shoulders and hips should be virtually level. Their lower back should not be drooping or arched. When their butt is too low, it will affect their pad level because they will be forced to stand up in their stance, which usually results in being knocked backward. If their butt is too high, they will fall or lunge out of their stance and be unable to sustain a block. We call that cannon fodder. They are just getting in the way of a defensive lineman for a split second but are not in proper position to execute a block.

If our last game is in mid-December, we will still be working with our linemen on their stances. You can't ever assume they will get it down. Players will often adjust their stance to accommodate an injury for example. These are teenagers. Even adults can get sloppy about tasks we've supposedly mastered.

Pre-Snap Routine
We've used the same cadence since 1979: "Down…Set…Hut."

Our linemen break the huddle and run to the line of scrimmage to prevent the defense from making adjustments. Then they adjust their splits, which is normally two-and-a-half feet between linemen. If we're running outside or if our linemen are anticipating a tandem or double-team block, we may narrow the splits. If we're confident we can get one-on-one blocks, we may widen them.

Once they get to the line and adjust their splits, we coach our linemen to place their hands on their knees because we want their heads up so they can see the defense and adjust accordingly. We do that in part because we have more running plays than most teams. We play good teams that may only have three basic running plays that can be run to either side. We have more than a dozen, and virtually all of them require our linemen communicate at the line of scrimmage.

On a basic option-veer play, for example, they have to decide which defender will be optioned and therefore who goes unblocked. On other plays they have to communicate whether to execute a one-on-one or a tandem block. We try to make the adjustments as simple as possible, but our linemen have to be able to recognize how the defense is aligned before knowing how to execute. When they come to the sideline after a series, they convey to us what they see on the field. This is a critical function of our ability as a coaching staff to make in-game adjustments. We make adjustments based on what they tell us they are seeing, and they can't do that if they are staring at the ground.

Once they are at the line of scrimmage and are reading and communicating, the quarterback will say "Down," and linemen will drop into their stance. The quarterback then says, "Set," followed by "Hut," at which point we fire off the ball with the goal of controlling the neutral zone. If those three commands can be executed quickly enough, it can become a thing of beauty. Opposing coaches have long complained about what they perceive to be our "rolling start," but that's not what we teach because it results in linemen diving or lunging off the ball instead of using the proper steps outlined later in the chapter.

If we're running a base play with straightforward assignments, we can drop directly into a set position and go on first sound to try to catch a defense off guard to add to the anxiety they may already feel about compensating for our speed and precision off the ball. So much of what we do is based on repetition. In order to get our linemen comfortable, we have them firing out of a stance to the sound of a quarterback's cadence from the first day we start our offseason conditioning program in January. Whether we're doing speed work, running gassers or 40-yard dashes, every time they come off the ball, it's to the sound of the quarterback's voice.

Each quarterback has a different cadence. Linemen must learn them all. We've tried to get our quarterbacks to have uniform cadences, but it never works. There's always something a little different from one quarterback to another. We always use the same "Down…Set…Hut…" snap count, so it's always the same progression.

Numbering System

We use our numbering system less and less because we keep seeing more exotic defenses, but it's a good starting point for veer and/or option plays because it simplifies our linemen's reads and gives us a structure to talk about assignments.

Imagine dragging a curtain across the field from the sideline. Whichever in-the-box defender the curtain hits first is No. 1, the next number is two, etc. If a defensive tackle and linebacker are stacked, we tell the kids to count the defensive lineman first. If we're running a straight option play, it means we're leaving a defender unblocked. In that case everybody blocks their number plus one. So the tight end would block the second defender, the tackle the third, etc. The first defender would be the player to be optioned.

There are exceptions. For example, on the option, the tight end and tackle can decide whether to block the defensive end or the outside linebacker. We want them to block whoever they think will be the easiest person to block. If the end is the inferior player, we tell them to block the end and we'll option the outside linebacker and vice versa.

Veer-option plays are triple options, and therefore we leave two defenders unblocked. The rule on a veer play is to block your man plus two, so the tight end would block the third defender, the tackle would block the fourth, etc. The No. 1 and No. 2 defenders are unblocked and would therefore be optioned.

Here's another rule we use to simplify things for our linemen while running veer or option plays: when in doubt step down. If you block all the inside guys and are getting off the ball, you have a good chance of getting yards. If you get confused and let an inside guy penetrate, you're in trouble.

Three-Step Technique

A three-step method is at the heart of our technique. As critical as learning those steps is to our linemen's success and our success as a team, we don't really focus on it until spring ball. If we did start to work on steps in January when we launch our offseason conditioning program, they wouldn't be able to do it. Even though we play our state championship game in mid-December, our junior varsity kids have been off since October. They're out of shape, and expecting them to execute those steps with the efficiency we demand is unrealistic.

We get off the ball so quickly because we drill it again and again until it becomes second nature. We once used the acronym BEEF—Blast off, Explode, Elevate, Finish—to describe this progression but have since streamlined it to three steps.

The first step has to be made by the play-side foot. If the play is going to the right, the right foot takes a quick, six-inch stab step in the direction of the defender's play-side foot. (Steps flat down the line are unacceptable unless the lineman is pulling because it's forward and not sideways momentum we are trying to create.) The step shouldn't be straight ahead unless the defensive lineman is head-up. The offensive lineman's hips have to be square to their target. If his toe is pointed straight at the defensive lineman's play-side foot, the hips will follow.

The second step is approximately 18 inches in length, depending on the distance between the opposing linemen. We tell our guys to get as deep as possible with the second step and to aim it at the midpoint between the defender's feet because the goal is to split his stance and therefore take away his power.

We also emphasize that their second step *must* be down *before* the defender gets his second step down in order to successfully complete the block. We can't emphasis this enough. Contact comes as the second step lands. If the offensive lineman's left foot is in the air on contact, he will get knocked backward. If he gets it down too quickly, his hips will be overextended and he will end up diving into his opponent.

Our philosophy is based on this truth: the lineman who gets his second step down first wins the neutral zone 100 percent of the time. Getting the second step down first gives the offensive lineman leverage to elevate the defender. Now all the momentum is on his side. He has effectively gotten leverage before the defender could complete his second step. The defensive lineman is vulnerable and in position to be moved off the line.

The second step is brutal. We spend 80 to 90 percent of our time coaching the second step. Sometimes we don't want to work on it or talk about it anymore, but it's absolutely essential to what we do. It's tedious for the kids and for us, but kids respond when they start to see results. Once they start getting their second step down first with consistency, their confidence and aggressiveness grow by leaps and bounds.

When our linemen make contact, we want their shoulder to be just a tick higher than their hips. We would love for them to be level, but that's pretty difficult. They should be close to level. Looking at a successful block from the side, the shoulders and hips should be close to level, the momentum should be going forward, and their feet should be underneath them. If that's the case and the head and shoulders and hips are all aligned, the player has become a battering ram, which is what we want.

A common mistake is made when players allow their rear ends to get below their shoulders. In that case the player loses pad level and therefore power. We also emphasize that the head and shoulders need to be in a straight line. We're always working in straight lines along the offensive line. We try to eliminate all wasted movement and keep their hips in proper position. We want them to stay compact, powerful, and in a straight line.

The third step is designed to put offensive linemen in position to either finish the block or move to a secondary defender and is accompanied by what we call "the Club". This step is also 18 inches in length and is to be followed by a series of quick finishing steps in man-on-man blocking to further drive the defender off the line of scrimmage. In many ways the third step doesn't matter. Blocks are won and lost in the first two steps. The third step is a natural follow-through. The only thing we really emphasize in Step No. 3 is hand placement.

The second step should be completed a split second before contact. If the first two steps are correct, the offensive lineman's facemask should be on the left side of the defender's chin with the top of his shoulder in his sternum. We always teach our linemen to hit with the top of the shoulder pad and not the front of it. It's just another way to emphasize the importance of proper pad level.

We call the moment they feel any sort of contact with their left shoulder "the hair trigger." That's when we bring "the Club," which is an old-fashioned type block, where the offensive lineman uses his forearm to deliver a blow to the defender's breastplate. The arm movement of "the Club" is the exact same as when performing cleans in the weight room. That's why we do so many reps of that kind of lift.

We tell the kids to pretend that their left hand is tied to their left hip. That way, when their arm moves forward, their hip moves forward. We don't want them cocking their arm any more than that because it's wasted movement. The arm should be bent slightly at about 75 degrees. As soon as they feel contact with the top of the left shoulder, the forearm and hips should come as far forward as possible, which elevates the pad level of the defensive lineman. To properly aim "the Club," they should aim the back of their hands at their opponent's crotch. The hand never actually hits the defender's crotch, but aiming for it helps maintain the proper pad level.

The first two steps create the battering ram that knocks the defensive lineman back and exposes his chest. If his chest is exposed, he has no hips. What we want as offensive and defensive linemen is to have our feet under us in a position of power. When we elevate them with "the Club," their hips are in front of their feet. They're useless in that position. At that point, even if our offensive lineman fell, his combatant

We emphasize sled work as a way to improve our straight-ahead and angle blocking. (Photo by Bob Larson)

could never make the tackle. All he could do is throw an arm out, and no running back should get tackled by that. If you can get a defensive lineman in this position, it doesn't matter what happens after that.

We emphasize this finishing position when we work on the sled. We tell them to bring their crotch to the blocking sled's pad while bringing their hips all the way forward. After contact we want them to thrust their hips forward as much as possible, which causes us to lift the sled into the air.

A lot of teams drive a sled. They hit it and lean on it and push it downfield. We never drive the sled. We have two sleds so we can split our linemen into two groups and we hit the sled using our three-step progression, which includes "the Club," between 50 and 100 times each practice, depending on how well we've been blocking. One group will go for six to eight reps, moving quickly before they go to the end of the line, and the second group does the same thing. We work on straight-ahead blocking and angle blocking. We might use the second sled to work on our pulling steps. The sled goes up, and it comes down. We reload and do it again, reload and do it again, reload and do it again. We don't drive our sled. We lift it and drop it. We knock it all over the practice field.

Pull-Blocking Steps

Pull-blocking steps begin with our linemen lightening their stances so more weight rests on the heels. We do *not* want our linemen leaning in their stances because this typically causes a crossover step, which robs him of his balance and includes too much wasted motion. They should also be careful not to rest too far back in their stances because doing so may tip off a defender.

The first step is vital because the lineman must drive off the instep of the non-pulling foot, rotate the pulling side elbow past his hip, and concentrate on opening his hips and pointing them toward the sideline. If this is accomplished, he will be in a proper pulling position, will not need a recovery step to put him back on track, and should arrive at the hole in a timely manner. All three points are essential to a quick, effective pull block.

Next, the lineman must reach full speed as quickly as possible to get to the hole. Once he approaches a defender, he must throttle down to get his body under control so he is not overextended. The focal point should be the lineman's shoulder being placed—while his head is up, of course—below the shoulder pads of the defender, while using the Club to follow through and create elevation. The pulling lineman finishes the block by driving his legs and working to block through the defender and thus creating a hole for the ball carrier.

Tandem Blocks

Our No. 1 play in recent years has been what we call "power" play, but most people refer to as "counter trey," which is the same play made famous by John Riggins and the Redskins on their Super Bowl teams. Former Redskins coach Joe Gibbs modeled this play after a similar one used by the Nebraska Cornhuskers.

It has become our top play in large part because we can run so much play-action pass off of it. We run play-action off our base veer plays, too, but are limited somewhat because on those plays the quarterback is running straight down the line of scrimmage rather than dropping straight back. It's a misdirection running play that often calls for the center, right guard, and tackle to back block or block the man to their left as if the play were going in that direction. Meanwhile, the left guard and tackle pull down the line of scrimmage. The running back feints left before cutting back to the right, receiving the handoff, and following the hip of the guard.

The defensive end is unblocked because the right guard and tackle are executing what we call a tandem block. Our success executing this block has made this play so effective that in the 2012 state semifinal and championship games we ran it at least 40 percent of the time.

Since this isn't a veer play, but one in virtually every team's playbook, the second most-asked question we hear is how we execute our tandem block. In this case our right guard and tackle are at least temporarily double-teaming the defensive tackle with the goal being to drive him inside, allowing the right tackle to detach from this initial block before moving upfield and attacking the middle linebacker, so the play can be run outside.

We try to keep our normal three-step progression as universal as possible. On this play, however, while the right guard takes his normal steps, we want the right tackle to double the normal length of his first step so that the right guard's right foot and the right tackle's left foot are side by side. If their feet are together, their shoulders should also be together. What kills a tandem block is when the defensive lineman splits the double-team. If our guard's and tackle's feet and shoulders are together, it's impossible to split that block, and the defensive lineman will be moved off the ball.

We tell our tackles to never leave the tandem block until the defensive lineman is moving back. If he's not, keep driving him. If he is moving back, the right guard will drive him back and end up on the defensive tackle's outside shoulder. That means the right butt cheek of the right guard will naturally slide the tackle off the block. As soon as the right tackle feels that slide, he should come off that block and attack the middle linebacker. He should have an advantageous angle to accomplish this.

It might sound as if this technique is easier described than executed, but our right tackle gets to the middle linebacker 75 percent of the time, which is high percentage in our mind, especially considering the middle linebacker often takes himself out of the play by getting faked out by the counter motion or boxed out by the defensive tackle who is being pushed into his lap.

We'll take that type of success rate every time.

Penetration by the defensive tackle and the middle linebacker are the biggest threats to properly executing this play. Those two defenders must be the focus of the offense for this play to be successful, and the tandem block takes care of them both, leaving the right guard and right tackle to release downfield and create a touchdown alley that can transform a routine running play into a game breaker.

Pass Blocking

Almost all of our pass blocking is predicated on play-action. For example, if we run a counter pass, or what we call a "power pass," where we're pulling a guard, our linemen are taught to get off the ball just like a running play but not to go to the second level and attack linebackers. We tell them to take their first three steps and throttle down. We still get a lot of illegal man downfield calls against us—not necessarily because we are illegally downfield—because officials aren't used to seeing offensive linemen play as aggressively as we do.

For us the old-fashioned umbrella pass-blocking schemes are a waste of time because 80 percent of our pass plays are play-action. We only pass about a fifth of the time, and only a fifth of those passes are traditional drop-back passing plays, so we don't spend a lot of time on traditional pass blocking. We prefer to spend the time getting our three-step technique down.

When we do run a traditional pass play, the center will read the defense and decide which way he is helping. If it's a "Larry" or "left" call, it means the center is helping to the left, and he and the left guard are responsible for the two inside guys on the left while the running back is helping out on the right side. We tell our linemen to keep their shoulders square and shuffle their feet, keep their elbows in, and punch and replace while pass blocking.

Quarterbacks
By De La Salle quarterbacks coach Mark Panella

I'm real honest with prospective quarterbacks. I tell them they are the focal point of a very well-known football team at a very well-known school. Win, lose, or draw, all eyes will be on them. Praise and criticism will fall on their shoulders, and they need to understand and accept that. They need to be able to take the heat.

We don't put a huge emphasis on quarterbacks winning games for us, but we make them aware that they can absolutely lose games for us, so the first thing they have to do is be a good game manager. That means making sure everybody is focused, getting in and out of the huddle with tempo, and communicating at the line of scrimmage.

If you're not very athletic, you can't play quarterback in our system. A couple years ago, we put the fastest kid in our school at quarterback. He always wanted to play the position, but he was too robotic, and we moved him to another position. You've got to be fluid to run the option.

The process of me getting to know our quarterbacks starts in earnest during the offseason. I'm an off-campus coach, but I talk to them when they're working out to get to know them personally. I treat the quarterbacks differently than I treat some of the other players. Very rarely do I yell at a quarterback, for example, because I don't want to usurp his authority in front of his teammates. I might take a walk with him down the sideline and let him know in no uncertain terms how I feel. But I don't want the rest of the team to think I don't have confidence in the quarterback because everybody's eyes are on him, especially in our offense. I might yell at a lineman: "What are you doing?" But I will not say that to the quarterback because if the coach doesn't show confidence in him, then his teammates won't have confidence in him when he steps into the huddle.

I like to watch our freshman and junior varsity team during games and practices to see how different quarterbacks react to coaches and their teammates. I might offer a coaching point to gauge how malleable they are so I have a better feel for them and how they learn when they join the varsity.

Mechanics

If I find something mechanically wrong with any of my quarterbacks, I immediately correct it. We're sticklers for it. It's the same for a lineman as the quarterback: if the first step is correct, everything falls into place. If the first step is outside of the frame, then you drag your second step, which means you're late getting back into the running back's fold, which affects the mesh point and creates fumbles.

We want our quarterbacks comfortable and relaxed under center, but we don't want them hunched over center. We want their backs straight. The center's back and the quarterback's chest should form a 90-degree angle. The quarterback's legs should be bent as if he is sitting in a chair, allowing him to lead with his hips and not his shoulders when the ball is snapped.

For the quarterback-center exchange, we want the throwing hand on top with the back of the throwing hand pressed against the center's crotch. The base of the thumbs of the throwing and non-throwing hands should touch. Once the exchange is secured, the quarterback should immediately seat the ball to his belt buckle.

Making sure the first step is inside the frame is the key to any running play. If the first step is too long, it's more difficult to get the second step down at the proper depth for the handoff. On our power play, or what others often call "counter trey," we have our quarterback open up to the hole side at 6 o'clock while immediately gaining depth away from the center so they don't collide with the pulling guards. We tell the quarterback to turn his back to the defense and hand the ball to the running back.

Every passing fundamental we teach has been adapted from Joe Namath's 1973 book, *A Matter of Style* with Bob Oates Jr. Lad gave it to me my sophomore year. It might seem odd that here in the Bay Area, where Bill Walsh coached and where Joe Montana and Steve Young played, that we're using a book more than 40 years old, but I believe in Namath's philosophy of minimizing movement. It's like a golf swing. The less movement there is, the less that can go wrong. Look at Dan Marino's old release. He patterned his throwing motion and release after Namath, too.

I've been complimented by coaches who say they love how deep and quick our quarterbacks get in their drop, but they can't get their quarterbacks to do it. I tell them it's pretty easy to do. It's just a different style than what is being taught today. We don't step and shuffle. Our quarterbacks turn their backs to the defense and run straight back because it creates more separation. Most coaches teach a shuffling dropback, but I like our guys to get away from the rush so they don't feel pressure. You can see downfield better that way, and it seems to time up better with our receivers since we throw a lot of longer, play-action passes.

Opening up, turning the hips, and running through the drop allows the quarterback to get a good break and plant leg. If you do it well, you should be on balance at the top of your drop, which is the goal. For a split-back veer team with a run-first mentality, we have put quite a few quarterbacks in college, so there's something to be said for it.

On the drop our first step opens up at 6 o'clock for both right and left-handed quarterbacks. Their toe should be pointed directly behind them, and their foot should be inside their frame. As the quarterback leads with his hips and goes from the set position to the 6 o'clock position, it should appear as if he is swiveling in a chair. We don't want a big first step because if the first step is outside the frame, the quarterback won't be able to get to the second step. Once that first step goes down, he immediately proceeds to the second step, which is as long as the quarterback can comfortably step on the same 6 o'clock line. The break step or second step acts like a javelin as all the weight goes onto the break leg, and the plant leg naturally falls into place, which constitutes the third step and should result in the quarterback being on-balance at the top of his drop.

Our five and seven-step drops include the same three steps outlined above. I spend 80 percent of my time working on a three-step drop because five and seven-step drops are natural extensions of the three-step drop. The first step is the same for all three drops, as is the break step, which is the fourth step in a five-step drop and the sixth step in a seven-step drop. The only difference is the quarterback is taking glide steps to gain depth (for steps two and three in a five-step drop and steps two, three, four, and five in a seven-step drop).

Because the quarterback's hips are parallel to the line of scrimmage, a glide step is just a natural running stride where the quarterback's hips are facing away from the line of scrimmage. In a perfect world, his shoulders would be perpendicular to the line of scrimmage so he can see at least half the field, but most kids aren't that flexible. We tell them if they have to turn their back on the defense, then they have to turn their back. That's just the way it goes.

More often, we use what I call a "quick seven" or a "quick five," which uses the same fundamentals but calls for the quarterback to execute his drop as quickly as possible and typically prevents him from getting the normal depth but can be advantageous with certain route combinations. Play-action passes comprise approximately 80 percent of our passing plays, three-step drops account for 15 percent, and five-step drops account for 5 percent. We only use the seven-step drop when we run a deep corner route.

For the throwing motion, once you're at the top of your drop, you should be in what I call an "athletic position," which means your feet are shoulder-width apart, and your knees are flexed. The ball should be chest high on what I call the "shelf" with the ball pointed out or down, whichever is most comfortable. The elbow should be relaxed and close to the body.

As the quarterback begins his throwing motion, a six-inch slide step slightly to the left of the target for right-handed throwers allows him to trigger his hips so his legs are part of the throwing motion. His hips should move parallel to the ground when they open. The front hip has to open so the back hip can follow through the target line. That's the bottom half or the bottom plane of the throwing motion.

As that's happening, the ball remains on the shelf. As the non-throwing hand comes away from the body, the knuckles of the throwing hand should be pulled to the sky so the ball comes up and out. What a lot of young quarterbacks want to do is drop the ball below the shelf, which creates an unwanted hitch in the throwing motion. If the knuckles are pulled toward the sky, when the ball comes up and out into the arm-angle slot, the elbow should be at or above the shoulder to create a 90-degree angle with the elbow being the fulcrum between the shoulder and the forearm/wrist. If the forearm is inside of 90 degrees the quarterback will lose power on his throw. If it's outside of 90 degrees, once his hips trigger, he will be putting too much torque on his shoulder, which could result in an injury.

When the quarterback's knuckles are pulled toward the sky, the front elbow of the non-throwing arm should get lifted until it is also pointing at the target, which ensures that the shoulders are on a second plane. As the ball is released and the hips open through the target line, the quarterback should pull hard on the front-side elbow trying to pierce his ribs with that front elbow, which forces the hips to turn and propels the ball up and out quickly, creating a tip in the shoulders and ensuring the shoulders are rotating on the second-level plane.

At the release point right after the ball leaves the hand, the quarterback's chest should be over his front knee. If his chest is behind his front knee, his release point is too far back. When done properly, there should be so much torque and follow-through that defenders should be able to read the name on the back of the quarterback's jersey after he releases the ball and completes his follow-through.

Mental Preparation

My goal is to empower the quarterback because if he's confident it will resonate in the huddle. I do a lot of mental prep with our quarterbacks to help take pressure off them. If I throw a lot of scenarios and if/ then statements at them during the preseason and leading up to the next game, then when they get on the field, they will have had time to process everything before it unfolds on the field.

It's more of an inquisitive discussion because I want to know what they're thinking so I can understand what they can do well, what they struggle with, and how much information they can take in at a time. I want to know their anxiety level, their pressure points. I need to understand all that so I can gauge their frame of mind and know how quickly we can install new schemes. Individuals have different learning levels, and it's my job to understand how quickly they adapt to change. With one quarterback I might say, "What do you think of this and this?" He'll say, "I love it. Let's do it." Then I know we can install something right away. For another guy it might be a two or three-week process, so I know I will have to introduce concepts much earlier.

Before spring ball starts, I make sure they have all the plays and have gone over them. They need to understand the depth of the routes, the timing, and distance of the pass plays. For running plays you just have to get out there and create muscle memory. With the passing game, there's more theory. They have to understand coverages and recognize what the defense is taking away and know what their reads are in various coverages.

After spring ball I sit them down, and we make goals. For example, if the team's goal is winning state, what do you have to do as a quarterback to get the team there? I want them to think about leadership qualities, being the hardest worker. You may not be the fastest or best athlete, but you can be the hardest worker. We had a quarterback a couple years ago who would always try to push his teammates. I told him he couldn't say those things because he was late to practice and last in gassers. Who was going to listen to him?

Once the season starts, I have the varsity quarterbacks over to my house on either Tuesday or Wednesday night. My wife cooks a big meal, and I try to gauge their mental state, work on leadership qualities, and prepare them for situations that might arise in the upcoming game. I ask questions such as, "How is the team feeling about the game? What's the mood of the team? Are there any problems on team, and what can you do as the quarterback to solve it in a non-threatening and non-offensive way?" I might give them a suggestion about how to pull a teammate aside and what to say.

Then we'll watch video, or I'll bring a grease board home, and we will mark it up. I'm always trying to put them in a specific situation. I might freeze the film and say, "It's third and long on the 20-yard line. What if we have this play called, and the corner lines up over there? What would you check to?" Questions like that help me understand what they're comfortable running because I always want them to check to something they like so they will be confident they can get it done. I ask a lot of probing questions like "Why would you do that?" There's no right or wrong answer. I just helps me understand how they think and where they are in their development.

We call the plays from the sideline, but I want to try to fit what's best for the athlete so he's more confident in what he's doing individually because it takes a confident quarterback to run an offense at its utmost efficiency.

Running Backs

By former De La Salle head coach Bob Ladouceur

We base a running back's success on whether or not he made the primary tackler miss or broke the primary tackler's tackle. In other words you can't let the first defender take you down. You always have to either make him miss or break a tackle. If you can't do that, you can't be an effective runner for us. Otherwise, I might as well be running the ball because I can go down as soon as I get hit, too.

To make yourself a great runner you have to break tackles and make people miss, and we've had some great ones like Patrick Walsh, Maurice Jones-Drew, and Lucas Dunne. Once you set that expectation, you look at the film and you can say, "The first guy took you down," and they will know exactly what that means. A defender will stick out an arm, and the ball carrier will trip over that arm. You can't let that happen when we train you to be prepared for that. We run those guys through the gauntlet to toughen them up to get them to get low and take on tacklers.

You have to have natural ability to play running back, but we develop our runners like we do all our players. By that I mean we teach them how to run the football and how to break tackles. When we watch game film on Saturday we watch every run, everything they are doing, whether they are carrying it with the wrong hand, and whether they're not play-faking right or loafing.

A lot of backs think they should be breaking runs on every play, but how many times do you see someone break a 50-yard run? It's rare. The key is: can you break some?

Dunne was a 5'9", 185-pound junior here a couple years ago. He was a fourth-quarter runner. When games got out of reach, I put him in there. He didn't know the plays well, ran the wrong way, used the wrong hand. He wasn't real tough but showed some promise. We pulled him aside after the season and told him we lacked a big-time running back the following year. We told him he could be a great runner, but he was lazy in the weight room and didn't always know the plays.

This kid bought in and put in an unbelievable offseason. He was in great shape. He was strong, ran the track hard, did his drills hard and

Running back Maurice Jones-Drew is one of the best players to ever don the Spartans uniform. (Photo by Bob Larson)

he went out and ripped up his senior season, setting school records with 2,043 rushing yards and 40 touchdowns. He may have broken more tackles than Maurice Jones-Drew. He is definitely one of our top three runners in history here, and it's because he drilled the right way, knew what was expected, bought into the philosophy, and worked hard to prepare himself. Guys like that are critical to your offense. I always tell our running backs that they have to be the toughest, hardest working, and best conditioned athletes on the team.

We've gained a ton of yards on our power play over the years. On that play our running backs line up at five yards directly behind the guards. The dive back receiving the ball sinks inside with his inside leg and receives the ball from the quarterback directly behind where the center originally lined up. The off back's first step remains inside the frame, and he points his inside leg directly at the pulling guard's outside leg. He then blocks the first man outside the guard.

If there was only one thing I could have my running backs do, it would be pulling tires because it simulates a power running position and power running posture and develops all the muscles you need to be a power runner. But here are other drills.

We do this drill more than any other. We have a center, quarterback, two running backs, two defensive bag men, and two read men who force the quarterback to read the defenders and make the appropriate play. We want the defenders to be in position to tackle our dive back or pitch back, even though we don't want them to take the ball carrier to the ground. We have them pop the running back with a chest protector or shield pad or they can make the initial hit. As always running backs are instructed to make the first man miss before accelerating and getting upfield as quickly as possible. The goal is for them to make a move on the defender and learn to run in space. Some guys only have one move or can only cut one way. This is a chance to develop other moves while also being monitored for ball security.

Our running backs run a gauntlet while doing position specific conditioning. The gauntlet starts with two players holding large stand-up bags. When the running back reaches the stand-up bags, he must lower his shoulder in an attempt to bust through the defenders. The resistance should be such that if he's running high they will stop him easily. If he has good body lean with his feet underneath him and his shoulders square, he should be able to bust through the stand-up pads, after which he is confronted with three players standing three yards from the sideline holding body shields. The running back has to stay in bounds while learning how to use body leverage to finish a run. The bag men try to knock the running backs out of bounds as they run past. Running backs are instructed to take those defenders on, bounce off, and break tackles using their right and left shoulders. We run the backs through one after another, and after 15 minutes, they're gassed.

Tight Ends

By current De La Salle head coach Justin Alumbaugh

The tight end is the most important blocker on our offensive line because two of our three most frequently used running plays—the outside veer and the power—require running behind the tight end. If our tight end can't get a push off the line and block in space, we're going to have trouble moving the ball.

Finding tight ends is difficult because they must know all the receiving routes and have the most complex blocking assignments on the team. Our tight ends must have the best feet of any of our linemen and a lot of toughness because he might need to block a linebacker stacked over him on one play, a defensive end on the next play, and a strong safety lined up outside after that. We may also require him to release inside and block a free safety.

We never look for a pass-catcher first. They are usually catching shorter passes, can use their bodies, and are often wide open on play-action passes, so if they have decent hands, we feel we can teach them to catch as they go along. If we can't find a natural tight end to fit our system, we move a tackle or guard to the position. We rarely use a pass-catching specialist because the blocking component is so important to our scheme and we pass so infrequently that it's obvious what we're planning to do if we were to send him into a game.

That's not to say our tight ends aren't involved in the passing game. Because our offensive line gets such a big push and gets to the second level so quickly it's difficult for defenders to know when our tight ends are attacking the second level as blockers or running routes because it looks the same. We use our tight ends to pressure defenses vertically, too, so they have to be savvy and know if a defender is trailing them or how to create space if they are playing man-to-man. We also will have him hold at the line for a few seconds before releasing into the flat.

Our tight end position averages 30 receptions over 14 games. In 2014 our top two tight ends averaged 22.2 and 16.5 yards per catch. We run two-tight end formations about half the time because it makes it difficult for the defense to know where we're going to run. In recent years our tight ends have been versatile enough to leave on the field when we go to four-receiver sets, which gives the offense a lot of versatility. Our tight ends are always involved in sled work. We also include them in one on ones and seven-on-seven drills as well.

||||||||||||||||||||||||||||||||||||||||||||||||||||||||||||||||||||||||||||||||||||||||||||||||||||||

Receivers

By De La Salle receivers coach Blake Tuffli

A De La Salle receiver is not just an athlete but a master and a technician of the craft of receiving. He gives maximum effort on every play regardless of the play type, game situation, or opponent. He will be physical off the press and crisp while running routes, will attack the football when making receptions, and will pride himself on frustrating an opponent with relentless physicality and effort in making touchdown blocks and the most of every opportunity presented in the passing game. Most importantly, he will dominate his opponent on every block. A De La Salle receiver must be selfless, knowing that few pass plays will be called during the game but that they will be of critical importance when they are called.

The stance and front step is much like a sprinter in the blocks. The inside foot is forward with the weight on the balls of the feet. The receiver should have 60 percent of his weight on his front foot and 40 percent on his back foot. Both knees should be bent with hips shifting down and back. The front knee should bend forward and be in front of the toes, and the back knee should be bent enough to prevent any drop in the height of the hips and shoulders on the snap of the ball. The balance should be strong and centered enough so as not to tip or stumble when pushed and pulled front to back and side to side. The receiver must be able to explode without wasted movement from this position and roll over the front foot and get the first step (with the back foot) down quickly. The hands must be in position to fight off the press but relaxed so as to remain smooth and fluid in both hand fighting and receiving the football. The stance must be emphasized on every rep of every drill and every play of practice and games because without the proper stance a receiver won't be in position to catch a ball.

We have a stance drill that focuses on centering. Receivers jog up to the line of scrimmage and get in their stance with inside foot up and eyes on the ball. We have them take a couple deep breaths from the diaphragm to center and balance themselves while in their stance. The coach should then go to each receiver and push or pull to ensure balance has been achieved. The coach should then step to the side and observe the receiver exploding out of his stance because balance without explosiveness is useless.

For the pre-snap routine and get off, you should have receivers jog to the line as if breaking from a huddle. Receivers should then use a pre-snap routine that includes identifying the coverage (even if there is none

Former De La Salle wide receiver Amani Toomer went on to a successful, 13-year career with the New York Giants. (Photo by Bob Larson)

during the drill), taking a deep breath as they get into their stance, and having a specific verbal cue that relates to the situation. Use a ball to focus on movement rather than cadence and use hard counts.

The Release

Releasing is a fluid art that takes a true feel. The same defensive back may not fall for the same move twice so adjustments may be required. When it comes to a release, our receivers have three options. 1) An inside release should be used on most inside breaking routes. 2) An outside release should be used on all outside breaking routes. This also applies to the fade when the route inside the fade is breaking to it. 3) A best release is what gets the receiver up the field the cleanest and fastest when no specific release is required.

All of these releases are vertical. The width a receiver loses or gains on any release should be no more than the width of the hash marks from his initial alignment. All releases against press coverage should be executed from a low, balanced stance. The receiver should only allow the defensive back to get his hands on the tops of his shoulder pads and should never allow the defender to get his hands on the receiver's chest. On all releases against press coverage, the receiver must use the defensive back's leverage and assignment against him by using *pressure*.

The receiver must pressure the defensive back in order to release vertically up the field. That pressure will cause the defensive back to either move his feet and therefore widen the vertical release window or stop his feet, lessening his leverage. Either will allow the receiver to explode through the defensive back's hip. For example, when the defensive back is playing inside eye press and the receiver has a fade route, the receiver must pressure upfield and inside through the outside shoulder of the defensive back to get the defensive back to move inside or stop his feet. The pressure causes the defensive back to lose leverage and power, allowing the wide receiver to hand fight and explode upfield vertically.

Releases that involve hand fighting require two primary combinations. The first is a hook to the elbow/bicep with the far hand striking forcefully the near arm of the defender. The second punch requires dipping the shoulder to keep the proper low pad level followed with an explosive uppercut through the hands of the defensive back. A quick swim keeping the elbow below the shoulder after the hook may also be used. The hook with a quick swim move will chop down the wrists and forearms of the defensive back. The hand fighting should begin after two or three hard steps have been made to put pressure on the defensive back. The two or three steps allow the receiver to have the proper foot planted to explode out of the hand fight vertically and off the hip of the defensive back. Inside releases are three steps, and outside releases are two steps.

After the second inside release using hard inside leverage, we want to "square them up and shake them." The receiver places more weight on the inside ball of the big toe on his back foot in this release to help him quickly step at a 45-degree angle toward the defensive back's inside foot. At the same time, the receiver must bring the back foot forward to the outside foot of the defensive back while remaining in an athletic stance. In basketball terms the receiver would now be in position to cross over the defender.

Our hand fighting drill is designed to increase comfort in stance and hand-fighting technique. Receivers should line up nose to nose a half yard from each other. The receiver playing the role of the defensive back for the purpose of this drill should stick both hands out in front as if he was thrusting to jam the chest area of the receiver with both hands. The defensive back's hands should touch the receiver while not holding him. The receiver then takes the proper steps and uses one of the two hand fighting techniques to release from the line of scrimmage. This drill should be done on both sides of the field with both the receiver's left and right foot in front.

The five-cone release drill is designed to practice stance and release versus press coverage. The receiver should practice inside and outside releases with both the left and right foot in front. Set up two cones two-and-a-half yards apart and two yards from the line of scrimmage. Set the third cone down eight yards from the line of scrimmage, splitting the difference between the first two cones. Set the last two cones five-and-a-half yards from the third cone. The receiver then jogs to the line of scrimmage and gets centered with the inside foot in front while watching the ball. On the snap of the ball, the receiver pushes the defensive back to the cone opposite his inside or outside release and uses one of the hand fighting techniques (always starting with the hook/uppercut). After exploding past the hips of the defensive back, the receiver should push vertically to the third cone while making sure the quarterback can see the back of his head. The receiver then plants, turns, and comes back to the ball (or runs a hitch, slant, out, or fade) and explodes upfield past the last two cones. Start the drill at walk-through pace and progress to full speed.

Catching

There are two basic ways to catch the ball. Both involve using the fingers with the palm only touching the ball after the fingers do. The body and arms should never be used to trap the ball. The ball should always be caught in front of the body to allow for the receivers to make the catch as they tuck the ball. The tip of the ball should be the focal point from the throw to the tuck with the eyes and head coming down when the ball is tucked.

If the ball is chest level or above, it should be caught with thumbs and index fingers touching while fingers are relaxed and spread like a spider's web. Elbows should remain bent and at approximate shoulder-width, allowing the thumbs to remain strong and the hands to greet the ball in front of the body, allowing space to absorb the momentum of the ball without the hands or ball touching the chest before the ball is tucked.

When the ball is below chest level, the receiver's pinky fingers should touch with the rest of the fingers spread and relaxed. Elbows should be bent and shoulder-width. Here are five drills to use to help hone the ability to catch:

- With a partner starting eight yards away, balls should be thrown high, low, left, and right while steadily increasing velocity. Receivers should focus on the tip of the ball through the tuck. (If you use balls with colored tips, the receivers should call out the color on the tip of the ball.) The receiver turns upfield after the catch.

- With a partner or in a group, have the receiver stand six to 10 yards away from the quarterback or partner with his back turned. On the quarterback's count, the receiver should break back to the ball as if doing a curl or comeback route. The receiver should plant on the opposite foot from the direction of the break with low hips, fast feet, and quick hands while making sure not to turn the head or shoulders early. This should be done with balance catching the ball using proper form. He should then tuck the ball and run upfield.

- Receivers should start 20 yards away from the quarterback before running in a straight line toward the quarterback. The ball should be delivered high, low left, and right with increasing velocity. The receiver should catch the ball using proper form and then make one sharp cut after catching the ball.

- Receivers start five yards in front and five yards to the left or right of the quarterback. The receiver will then simulate cutting and exploding out of the break looking to catch the ball. The quarterback fires the ball in directly out of the break or after the receiver has taken several strides while placing it high, low, in front, and behind the receiver, who catches the ball, tucks it, and explodes up the field. This drill can be done with distractions such as a linebacker in the window or striking the receiver immediately after the catch with a bag or another player passing in front of the receiver during the catch.

- Have receiver take off at full speed on a fly route for 10 yards. The quarterback then throws the ball to the back shoulder and high, forcing the receiver to stick his outside foot in the ground and attack the ball like a rebound. The ball should be caught above the head of the receiver and tucked immediately.

Blocking

These three basic blocks must be executed with a controlled but aggressive attitude.

In the stalk block, hips should remain square to the line of scrimmage. When the receiver strikes the defensive back, it should be in a low to high movement with the hips opening and the palms striking the chest plate in a technique similar to how we ask our offensive linemen and linebackers to strike. In fact, we drill our receivers on the blocking sled similar to the linebackers and offensive linemen to reinforce how similar the techniques are. The goal of the stalk block is to drive the defender back to create a bigger running lane for the running back. There should be minimum possible space between the receiver and the defensive back to decrease the odds of a holding penalty. We tell our receivers to try to step on the toes of the defender.

We employ the crack block when trying to get to the perimeter of the defense quickly via tosses or swing passes. The first step is a flat step parallel to the line of scrimmage. If the linebacker or safety comes upfield fast toward the line of scrimmage, the receiver has a better angle to keep his head in front and avoid a clip. After starting flat and parallel to the line of scrimmage, the receiver should adjust his angle to ideally be working upfield and exploding into the defender while keeping his head in front. The receiver on contact will explode from low to high, and his hips will open and thrust after the initial strike. The receiver should deliver the blow—not absorb the blow. If he is assigned to crack a player and that player blitzes, the receiver is to work inside and up the field and pick up the first linebacker or safety who shows himself.

Any play to the opposite side of the field requires the receiver to take a flat step and then release across the field with the goal of picking up the play-side outside linebacker. This rarely happens against a well-coached team, but the receiver often ends up with good angles for blocks on free safeties and others if the runner reverses field. This block is more about a mentality. On every play, no matter how far away, you can be a vital part of the success of the play if you work hard and have an aggressive attitude.

IIIIIIIIIIIIIIIIIIIIIIIIIIIIIIIIIIIIIIIIIIIIIIIIIIIIIIIIIIIIIIIIIIIIIIIIIIIIIIIIIIIIIIIIIIIIIIIIIIIIIIIIIII

Veer

By De La Salle quarterbacks coach Mark Panella

The split-back veer offense is a triple-option that features three potential ball handlers—quarterback, the dive back, and pitch back—and two unblocked defenders at the point of attack, thus giving the offense a numerical advantage. The quick-hitting offense relies on an aggressive offensive line that create creases instead of sustaining blocks before moving to the second level. It also requires superior ballhandling by the quarterback, quickness at the running back positions, and one-on-one blocking by the wide receivers.

The staples of the offense are inside and outside veer option plays. Perfecting those two basic components requires hours of tedious, monotonous repetition. Fundamentals and footwork are paramount to success, which is a big reason why we spend so much time on those two areas. It's not an offense you can easily illustrate on a grease board or show players via film. You need to be on the field running it again and again to create the required muscle memory.

A fire hose is one of our most important tools. It's painted to reflect the two-and-a-half foot splits between the center, guards, tackles, and tight end, so our quarterback and running backs can work on their precise steps without an offensive line and without pads.

We also make sure we have two defenders holding bags whenever we run our inside and outside veer plays because we want to give the quarterback the most realistic experience possible so he is accustomed to reading defenses.

One bag man plays defensive tackle and is told to take either the dive back or the quarterback, which forces the quarterback to read that defender. The stand-up bag man, who represents either a defensive end or an outside linebacker, commits to either the quarterback or the pitch back, forcing the quarterback to make a second read. We never practice the inside and outside veer plays without bag men. That's how critical the quarterback's read is to the success of the offense. We also move the bag man around to simulate different defensive looks he may see during the season. We also run as many up-tempo plays as possible during these sessions because the goal is to put players in a stressful or game-like situation. We want them fatigued when we finish to help make the reads, steps, and ballhandling less of a conscious effort and more of a natural reaction. Despite all the repetition, it typically takes a

Two of our potential options in the split-back veer offense are ready for action. (Photo by Bob Larson)

quarterback four games in the offense before he starts to get a feel and therefore the game slows down for him. The more you do it, the sooner the light bulb comes on, and you see the reads, the blocks, and the linebackers flowing, but it's a result of the competition.

Inside Veer

On an inside-veer play, the quarterback should read the down defensive lineman just outside the offensive guard. If the defensive lineman steps down and closes the hole, the quarterback should keep the ball. If he remains outside, the quarterback gives the ball to the dive back. If the defensive lineman steps down to engage the running back, the quarterback should let the dive back pass before immediately attacking the inside shoulder of the outside linebacker/defensive end with the goal of making him commit to the quarterback or the pitch back. If he commits to the quarterback, the quarterback pitches to the pitch back. If he commits to the pitch back, the quarterback keeps the ball and runs upfield inside the defender's inside shoulder.

On an inside-veer play to the right, the quarterback—after placing the football at his belt buckle—makes his first step inside the frame at 3 o'clock when running to the right. (It's 9 o'clock when running to the left.) The second step is parallel to the line of scrimmage as long as it can be made comfortably. The quarterback should then chatter or chop his feet as the dive back comes through the mesh point.

Both backs should line up four yards behind the line of scrimmage directly behind the guard in front of them. The dive back's first step is a six-inch directional step directly toward the play-side guard's outside leg. His eyes should be up, and he should be looking downfield and not at the quarterback. If he looks at the quarterback, he will slow down. This is a game of trust. The dive back must trust the quarterback will make the right read. The running back then runs through the mesh point with a soft fold so the quarterback can pull the ball as the read dictates. If the quarterback rides the mesh point past his upfield leg, the running back should grab the football. If the quarterback hasn't made up his mind by then, the dive back should take the ball and run to daylight.

The pitch back's first step is with his inside foot at 3 or 9 o'clock. He should then cross over with his other leg and run as fast as he can while maintaining a relationship of four yards away and four yards in front of the quarterback, which allows him to catch the pitch while running downhill toward daylight. The pitch back's goal is to get to the third level as soon as possible, where he will have a one-on-one with the free safety if everyone executes their blocks.

Outside Veer

After placing the football at his belt buckle, the quarterback's first step is 1 o'clock or 11 o'clock moving downhill to the mesh point, which is located a half yard to a yard past the line of scrimmage (depending on how quickly the offensive line gets off the ball) and just outside the tackle's outside leg. That immediately puts pressure on the defensive end. If he's outside the tight end, the quarterback is to attack his inside shoulder. The second and third steps are a sprint to the mesh point as fast as possible. Unlike the inside veer, the quarterback does not ride the dive back. He either hands him the ball or not. If he does not, the quarterback immediately goes to his second read, which is typically the strong safety, the free safety, the outside linebacker, or whoever is the second man in from the sideline (counting the cornerback).

The quarterback should attack that man's inside shoulder to force him to commit to either the quarterback, in which case the quarterback pitches to the pitch or dive back. The dive back's first step is a six-inch directional step toward the play-side tackle's outside leg before proceeding to the mesh point. If he receives the handoff, he should run to daylight. The pitch back's first step is with his inside leg at 3 or 9 o'clock. He then crosses over with his other leg and runs as fast as he can while maintaining a distance of four feet wide and four feet in front of the quarterback while awaiting a pitch.

The play-side wide receiver blocks the cornerback in front of him. The receiver opposite the play releases downfield with the intention of blocking the free safety. This is as tough of a block as there is in our offense. However, the assignment requires maximum effort because the opposite receiver could be in ideal position to block the free safety if the ball carrier cuts back. If not and the free safety is unreachable, he should turn and block the opposite cornerback.

CHAPTER 5

Defense

We're going to eliminate the big play and make the offense earn everything they get.

—De La Salle defensive and special

teams coordinator Terry Eidson

We've taken great pride in our defense through the years. We feel you cannot have a championship-caliber team unless you play great defense. Offense may be more exciting, but defense is the soul of your team. I was an offensive varsity assistant for seven seasons before being named the varsity defensive coordinator in 1992. When the time came to choose a defensive philosophy, I spent a lot of time thinking about what gave my offenses fits.

Our veer attack produces a lot of big plays. It's an offense designed for quick strikes in the running game that set up deep, play-action passes. As disciplined as our offense is, making it drive the length of the field often results in turnovers, penalties, missed assignments, and turning the ball over on downs. Driving the ball methodically down the field is difficult for any offense, so I decided to design a defense that forced teams to do exactly that.

I settled on a base 4-4 because of its balance and simplicity. Stopping the run is paramount at the high school level, and it's difficult to run against a 4-4, even if you don't see it much anymore. That's even true for teams that run spread offenses, which have become increasingly popular in recent years. Some look at spread offenses as passing offenses, but its primary function is to spread out opposing defenses to make it easier to find running lanes. Even against spread teams, the 4-4 allows us to cover the front seven while keeping the inside linebackers inside, splitting the outside linebackers out with two safeties behind in what remains a balanced defensive set against virtually any offense. It has been effective for us as we have allowed only 11 points per game and posted 74 shutouts since I became defensive coordinator in 1992.

Sometimes coaches tell me they had to switch to a 3-4 defense because they don't have enough quality defensive linemen. That's understandable. I remember in 2004, the season our 151-game winning streak ended, we had to stand a defensive lineman up because we were shorthanded. For the most part, however, it hasn't been a problem for us because we don't look for prototypical defensive linemen. We play with guys who weigh 190 pounds. We look for tough kids who are strong.

We can take almost anybody and make them a defensive lineman if they learn our technique and are tough kids.

Our defense is a read-and-attack defense. We don't penetrate. We're going to attack the blocker in front of us, control the line of scrimmage, move laterally up and down the line, and scramble to the ball. As a change-up we will crash gaps, but we make our living hitting and reading. We are hard to run on because there's nowhere to run. Running backs are used to seeing penetrating linemen, which makes it easier to find running lanes. When they play us, they typically find green jerseys.

Our philosophy is to make running backs stop their feet and bounce outside where our outside linebackers are waiting for them. On outside runs we are physical at the point of attack and try to force running backs to the sideline. Our core philosophy is simple: we're going to be excellent tacklers, our scheme will be simple so we play with confidence, we're going to eliminate the big play and make the offense earn everything they get.

I try to force offenses to throw to the outside, for example, because those are the most difficult throws to complete at the high school level. Our offense can't even complete them half the time. Running an inside pattern requires an easier body movement. When you run an out route, you have to get your shoulders and head turned. The timing is difficult. Plus, it's the toughest throw of all for a quarterback. If you're on a hash mark in high school, the throw is shorter, but if you're in the middle of the field, it's more difficult to execute because it takes a big-time arm to complete that pass. That's why I usually shade my guys to the inside to guard against inside routes. I'm giving up the outside routes, but not many of those get completed against us.

We've seen virtually every type of offense over the years, including ones that were designed for success against us. There's no situation where an offense can outman us because we have that balance. The only thing that consistently exploits our defense is a quarterback rolling out with the tight end, which is rare these days. We play our defensive ends on the inside shade of the tight end in a seven-technique, so when the quarterback rolls out it's easier to pin our end.

How we combat that is we tell our inside linebacker on that side to immediately engage the quarterback when he breaks contain, and our other inside linebacker replaces him. We constantly stress to our outside linebackers and defensive backs to remain in coverage until the quarterback has passed the line of scrimmage.

The biggest mistake I see from coaches is making their defense too complicated for their kids to play aggressively. Any defense can be effective as long as there are simple rules, you constantly drill players on their technique, and the players know what they're doing. Design a few simple rules, make sure the kids know them, and live and die with them. The simpler it is, the more confidence they will have. And the more confident they are, the more aggressive they become, and it takes a lot of aggression to play defense effectively.

The difference between what we do and what a lot of other programs do is not our philosophy so much as how we teach. You can run the same defense somewhere else, and it could get ripped. Why is this happening? I can show you right away. It's because of the technique of the linemen and how the linebackers play. It's not necessarily that our philosophy is better than anybody else's philosophy. Any scheme can work if you have the players, and they are confident and they know what they're doing. It's not about a particular philosophy but a coach's ability to teach that specific philosophy and get what he wants from his players. A coach may want to emulate what we do, but it's not going to work unless he can teach our technique. That's been the difference. It's about breaking it down step by step. Their footwork is so important. You have to hold them to a standard you want them to reach until they get there. I tell our kids all the time that, while it seems like you're not doing anything right, we're trying to teach you, and part of that is when you make mistake after mistake you learn from it. Be happy your coaches want you to be the best you can be.

Once a coach stops correcting a player, it means he doesn't think he can do it. We tell our kids half the battle is listening and not making excuses. Growth as a person and a player only occurs when we learn from our mistakes. We constantly remind our players that if they are coachable, good things will happen, and they do.

We're up-front with our kids. We tell them straight out that you have to be involved with high-speed contact to be a good defensive player. It's not the same as playing offense. A running back can run out of bounds. An offensive skill position player's job is to *avoid* being hit. Defensive players don't have that luxury. They have to *love* contact. That means a willingness to push their bodies. They have to be able to tolerate the discomfort that comes with defensive collisions. Running into people full speed goes against human nature. To prepare for this, we want them in the best shape possible. Our lifting and running program is

Coach Terry Eidson instructs the defensive players, who run his 4-4 scheme. (Photo by Bob Larson)

demanding and arduous. We don't push players to be sadistic but rather to help them be safe and successful.

Time spent in the weight room and conditioning helps players become naturally aggressive. Putting in all that time and all that work during the offseason gets their strength and speed up and boosts their confidence. We put them through the ringer because it gets them in great shape, but it also creates an attitude. They feel like they have spent a lot of time preparing for a game and they want to play with maximum effort on the field. We do not tolerate a player standing and watching when the play is away from him. You are not being accountable to your teammates when you do that. We expect our players to fly around the field on every play. Effort and hustle are demanded on every play, and we condition with that in mind. I flat out tell them if they don't like contact, if they can't tolerate pain and they can't push themselves the way I need them to, go play offense.

Blitzing

We're going to make you earn it, and that means preventing big plays, which is why I don't blitz much. Another factor in this approach is that many of our defensive players also play offense. Because I don't have them to myself all week, I don't want our defense to be too complicated. Confusion leads to touchdowns.

When we do blitz, we play a lot of man-to-man, and everybody has to know who they have. You wouldn't think man-to-man would be complicated, but many times I have blitzed over the years only to have a receiver go uncovered. Invariably, many of the long plays we have given up over the years have been the result of blitzes.

In recent years, so many teams are playing man-to-man that our zone schemes cause problems for quarterbacks because they don't see them often. I only blitz when I feel like we need it. I've had coaches ask me if there's a specific down and distance on the field when I like to blitz. The answer is no. In general, I blitz for one of three reasons.

- If I see our defense being too passive on the field, I will blitz to make them aggressive.

- I blitz when I have to disrupt what the other team is doing offensively because what we're doing isn't working.

- I blitz when our base, slants, or crashes on the defensive line aren't working.

The best time to blitz is when they don't expect it, which is often during a down and distance when I haven't blitzed before. You have to self-scout and know when they expect you to blitz. If the opponent is a team we play every year, I can watch film and remind myself when blitzing was and wasn't successful the last time we played. If they know when you're going to do it, it's not as effective. You have to think about what you ran against them and what they ran against you. You have to think about what they think you're going to do. What do they like to run in certain down and distances or in a certain area of the field? When inside the 10-yard line, a lot of teams run plays that are good blitz beaters, which means that's not the time to bring the heat. You have to get a read on the team and what they want to do. It's a chess match in that sense.

I call maybe five to eight blitzes a game, but it depends on how the game unfolds. If an opposing offense is trying to get rid of the ball fast because they don't think their offensive line can hold our defensive line, what's the point? Sometimes opposing offenses change the way they play against us. They may be a five to seven-drop passing team or a deep shotgun team, but against us we only see three-step drops. If that's the case, it doesn't make sense to blitz. Remember, your job as a defensive coach isn't to outsmart the opposing coach. Your job is to put your players in position to succeed.

|||||||||||||||||||||||||||||||||||||||||||||||||||||||||||||||||||||||||||||||||||||||||||||||||||

Defensive Line

By De La Salle defensive line coach Steve Jacoby
and former De La Salle head coach Bob Ladouceur

Defensive linemen must know their alignment, assignment, and technique in our base, pass, stunt, blitz, and goal line defenses. Defensive linemen attack blockers to prevent them from making forward progress by stepping, striking, and extending their arms while remaining square to the line of scrimmage, maintaining gap responsibilities, and not penetrating past the heels of the offensive linemen unless in pass rushing mode. The goal of defensive linemen is to win the neutral zone and force running backs to go where they don't want to go. If you can reroute the runner with the front four, you have a much better chance of stopping him for no gain. We want to build a wall that is square to the line of scrimmage. Therefore, we want to clearly see the numbers of our defensive linemen when we're watching end zone film.

We do not watch the ball. We watch the player across from us. If he moves, we move. We don't want our defensive ends looking down the line at the ball when they should be reading the guy in front of them. On all our sled progressions, we have an injured player or one of the players waiting his turn stand between the pads in the middle of the sled. As that person counts cadence, they step forward like an offensive lineman, and the defensive linemen react to his movement.

We emphasize *step, strike, and extend.* The following progression is taught to all defensive linemen and is best perfected in progession by first walking players through it, going live on a four-man sled, live on a one-man sled, and then live against offensive linemen in one-on-one drills. We're in a four-point stance with hands and toes all touching the ground. We want their hips higher than their shoulders and their feet underneath them. Their hands and feet should be closer together than an offensive lineman. If their shoulders are higher than their hips, we've found defensive linemen have a tendency to stand up. If their hips are higher, their contact point will be lower, and they can nullify their charge and stand the offensive lineman up.

As soon as the defensive lineman senses movement, we want him to violently strike the opponent's breastplate with his hands, which should occur at the same moment that his facemask collides with the facemask of his opponent. This should also coincide with two forward steps being executed. Whatever side we shade to, that foot is always the foot that starts back. The footwork begins with a stance where the toes of the back foot line up with the middle of the front foot. The first step with the back foot is 10 to 12 inches, and the second step with the front foot should result in the feet being almost even and shoulder-width apart. These steps must be taken as quickly as possible, and then feet should be chopped to maintain power and leverage.

The defensive lineman's eyes should be below the offensive lineman's eyes at all times. His thumbs should be turned in and the elbows out. We don't want him winding up or recoiling his hands before striking. Hands should go from the ground to the strike position to prevent offensive linemen from getting a clear path to the body. We exaggerate these movements when going against air or machinery, so when we go against real players, we have such a good foundation that all the coaches do is tweak and/or fine-tune technique. The perfect result of this drill is the defensive lineman's hips are thrust forward, and he's fully extended, working from low to high with his hands super extended and his biceps near the offensive lineman's earholes.

You can reload and do that against the sled two or three times. Depending on your shade, your right or left foot is back, and we work equally with both. Now that we've worked on our hand strike we want to incorporate a great stance against air and machinery, and then the second part of our progression is our strike and two steps coming together until they fully lock out and elevate the sled so their knees are slightly bent and their hands are above their eyes. We just take our two steps so we don't drive the sled. We strike it, square it up, elevate it, and chop our feet.

If the left hand ends up with a handful of jersey, the hand strike was too high. Now the lineman is hanging on and not being a striker. Other common mistakes are the eyes not being below the offensive lineman's eyes, a poor strike, a failure to extend, and a failure to execute their steps properly, which are coaching points that can be made quickly to maximize repetitions.

Pass Rush

We don't believe a defensive lineman can rush efficiently if he's in run mode. It's too difficult for them to be thinking about stopping the run and somehow transition into being an effective pass rusher. Coaches have to do their due diligence and call for a pass rush defense in pass rushing situations. We call it "Jet." When that Jet call is made, kids loosen up their alignments and stances.

We tell our defensive linemen to bull rush the offensive linemen first. We want them to drive the offensive lineman into the quarterback just to see if they can do it or what kind of resistance they will get. It gets the offensive lineman thinking this is what the defensive lineman is going to do every time. It's also a test. Let's see how tough that guy is, how strong he is, and how well he moves his feet. Let's see if he holds his ground. If they can bull rush effectively, we tell them to stick with it and try to force that lineman into the lap of the quarterback.

If the offensive lineman holds his ground, the defensive lineman has to think about a different pass rush mode. If that's the case, I want our defensive linemen thinking about what move they are going to use. Push pull? Arm under? Arm over? False step? They need to have a plan. It needs to be recognizable. I don't want them flailing around, trying this or that. I want to recognize the technique they are attempting to employ. Kids have a tendency to start hand fighting, and then they're not thinking about getting to the quarterback or how to defeat the guy in front of them. The focus has to be on getting to the quarterback. When I critique my pass rushers while watching film, it always starts with my ability to identify their plan of attack.

It's also important that linemen maintain the integrity of their pass rush lanes, which are usually the same as their run lanes. I always tell my guys that they are rushing the passer in a tunnel. They can line up in an opposite gap and use a false step as long as they cut back to their original rush lane. If they choose another rush lane or take the path of least resistance, it can create a gigantic hole that the quarterback can run through.

Most quarterbacks are runners these days. If they get past the line of scrimmage, they are going to pick up first downs, and that can be demoralizing. We tell our outside rushers that their primary responsibility is contain. We don't want the quarterback to get flushed out of the pocket by our inside guys if our outside rushers aren't in position to contain. We don't want our outside guys to cut underneath and risk getting pinned inside unless they are absolutely sure they can get to the quarterback. Likewise, we don't want them to be deeper than the quarterback and we don't want them getting washed or propelled past the quarterback by the offensive tackle. That's as bad as cutting underneath because it opens a lane.

As for pass rush principles, we tell our kids to keep their shoulder pads lower than their opponent because it creates more force and momentum. We also preach that they have to chop up or down to keep the offensive lineman's hands off his breastplate. Once the offensive linemen gets his hands on your breastplate, you're done. Hand speed and hand fighting are critical. Another good technique is a stab, where the defensive linemen extends an arm to the top of the offensive lineman's breastplate. The offensive lineman has less to grab onto when a defensive lineman executes a one-arm stab. All pass rushing techniques have some validity, though we discourage spinning. It can work occasionally if the lineman is athletic enough, but as a staple, it's not effective because the offensive lineman can get his hands on his back and wash him out of his lane.

We constantly remind our defensive linemen to keep their eyes on the quarterback. When we drill our pass rushers, and we do that often, we always use a live quarterback and have him move in the pocket. We want the quarterback to feel the pressure and try to escape. We want our defensive linemen to get used to that. That's when they get their sacks.

Base Defense

Ninety percent of the time, if not more, we're in our regular 40, Cover-1 defense. What we determine to be the strong and weak side changes from week to week based on the opponent and scouting reports. For example, if the offense is running a double tight end formation with a wingback to one side, we would designate the side with the wingback as the strong side, and our three-technique would line up accordingly.

Our one-technique lines up on the inside shade of the weak-side guard with his outside eye on the guard's inside eye. Remember, whatever side we shade to, that foot is always the foot that starts back. In this case, the right foot would be back and would be lined up with the middle of the left foot with the feet a little wider than shoulder-width. The responsibility of the one-technique is to own and maintain the A gap. Nobody should push him off the ball. If a ball carrier should run into A gap, he should own the play or force the ball carrier to bounce outside.

The three-technique tackle lines up on the outside eye of the strong-side guard with his left foot back and lined up with the middle of the right foot. The three-technique tackle's responsibility is to own and maintain the B gap. If the running back sees him owning the B gap and runs outside, the three-technique has done his job, and the ball carrier becomes the linebacker's responsibility.

Likewise, our seven-technique lines up on the inside eye of the tight end and owns the C gap. If the tight end arc releases or releases away,

Our coaches ensure our defensive linemen employ the proper technique out of a four-point stance. (Photo by Bob Larson)

the seven-technique should immediately look to the inside in an attempt to shut down a run to the spot vacated by the tight end. Teams have tried to attack us that way in recent years. They have also tried to use wider than ordinary splits to create gaps via alignment against our base defense.

Our six-technique lineman lines up on the outside eye of the weak-side tackle. He should be squeezing the B gap and owning the C gap in an attempt to make the ball carrier bounce outside of either gap. Once a running back has been forced to reroute, defensive linemen are to immediately scramble to the ball using proper angles of pursuit. A failure to hustle by one defensive lineman can cause a huge running lane.

If we're in our base defense and we anticipate a pass play, our run gap assignments are also our passing lane assignments. If the three-technique has B gap in the base defense, his rush lane is through the B gap. It's the same with the one-technique and the A gap. If the tight end arc releases, our seven-technique's pass rush lane is C gap, and he also has outside containment responsibilities. The six-technique comes off that offensive tackle like he does in the base defense and has containment on his side. When we're in pass mode, we really stress that if our three-technique or our one-technique gets double-teamed, the tackle with the one-on-one matchup is obligated to beat his man and get to the quarterback every time.

Blitz and Goal Line

When we're in our regular 40 mode, every defensive lineman has a gap responsibility. The biggest difference when we're in stunt/blitz mode is we're telling them where to go automatically. Instead of reading the play, they should get off the ball and get upfield as quickly as possible to execute their designated responsibility and create a push upfield that allows our twists and stunts to work. If we run a twist we call "ET," the end goes first and the tackle second. "TENT" means the tackle is first and the end second. If the offensive lineman picks them up, the blitzing defender or stunt partner should be free. If the offensive lineman picks up the blitzing defender or stunt partner, the defensive lineman should be free.

Our goal line scheme is simple. We bring in extra defensive linemen. The general rule is if the quarterback is under center we're going to play the center tighter. The tackles would line up with their inside shoulders on the outside shoulders of the center. If the quarterback is in shotgun, we widen out toward the guard and play the gap. The one and three-techniques are responsible for A gap. We have two defensive linemen in B gap and we bring in an extra defensive lineman to the strong side of the formation in C gap.

||||||||||||||||||||||||||||||||||||||||||||||||||||||||||||||||||||||||||||||||||||||||||||||||||||||||||

Linebackers

By De La Salle head coach Justin Alumbaugh

A confident, aggressive corps of linebackers is essential to the integrity of our defense. We typically allow at least one linebacker to roam sideline to sideline and make plays. Linebackers are expected to cover the pass and aggressively stop the run. For our system, specialty or hybrid players are not encouraged.

Aggressiveness is essential for our linebackers, and you can't be aggressive if you're not confident. Confidence comes from having the ability to properly execute the skills we demand of our athletes, which can be demonstrated during the offseason and during training camp. Linebackers must also have in-depth knowledge and understanding of the opposition's tendencies and the playbook, which is the product of intensive study of film and scouting reports. Those who have not displayed confidence, aggressiveness, and a mastery of the necessary skills are not allowed to play.

Reads

De La Salle linebackers read blockers. People ask us about run fits with the A and B gaps. We don't believe in that. Our inside linebackers read the guard in front of them, and our outside linebackers read the tackle or tight end. The only run fit we care about is where the ball carrier is.

It is the linebacker's coach's job to make sure players fully understand the following reads because to be most effective it's essential that linebackers execute these reads with aggression and without hesitation. If the guard straightens or pops up, the inside linebacker should immediately drop into coverage, keeping his head on a swivel and attacking the nearest receiver. If the guard attacks the defensive line or fires off the ball, the inside linebacker should step up and read the center and tackle. He should then attack either the center or the tackle, depending on who is attacking them. If the guard pulls, the inside linebacker should run through the head of the tackle. If he's pulling on an inside running play, he should go through the center's hole because linebackers should never be pinned inside on a running play. By placing his inside shoulder on the outside shoulder of the blocker, the linebacker will have the leverage he needs.

If the tackle or tight end straightens or pops up, the outside linebacker should immediately drop into coverage, keeping his head on a swivel and attacking the nearest receiver. If the tackle or tight end fires off the ball, the outside linebacker should step up and read flow. If flow is coming his way, he should attack any blockers headed his way. If the flow goes away, the outside linebacker should guard against the bootleg before joining pursuit.

Technique

The linebacker's primary responsibility is to attack and defeat a blocker because offensive players are designed to block them on every play. We drill our linebackers daily in what we call the butt-up drill. We put three or four bags on the ground several feet apart that linebackers must step over laterally while keeping their shoulders square to the line of scrimmage. This is to reinforce the importance of keeping the knees and feet high while moving laterally. When the linebacker steps over the fourth bag, the offensive lineman standing two yards to the side and two yards back charges at him full speed with another bag in an attempt to knock him on his butt, which occurs frequently.

The linebacker is instructed to attack the offensive lineman's inside shoulder with his near shoulder to ensure that his hips are square to the target. Similar to an offensive lineman, if the linebacker's hips are not square, he is not in the proper position to defeat the blocker.

The linebacker should strike the lineman with the front of his near shoulder while using his forearm to deliver a blow to the offensive lineman's breastplate. When the top of the shoulder makes contact, the hips come through, and the right hand comes forward with thumbs up and elbow brushing the ribcage and extending all the way through to the chest plate to create elevation. The linebacker should then shed the lineman to the inside or outside, depending on the route of the ball carrier before clearing the backside foot to the heel of the offensive lineman and attacking the ball carrier. In other words linebackers should either immediately force the running back to cut inside or string him toward the sidelines.

||||||||||||||||||||||||||||||||||||||||||||||||||||||||||||||||||||||||||||||||||||||||||||||||||||||||

Defensive Backs

By De La Salle defensive and special teams coordinator Terry Eidson and De La Salle secondary and special teams/kicking coach Donnie Boyce

We employ an aggressive, attacking secondary that physically challenges receivers at the line of scrimmage but plays primarily a zone scheme. We don't play a lot of man-to-man except in certain situations, such as third and medium because teams like to run crossing routes and pick routes when facing that down and distance, and jamming receivers at the line of scrimmage disrupts those routes. Those quick, inside routes are more difficult to cover when we're in a zone. We don't do a lot of rotating or man-to-man/zone combinations because we don't want our guys thinking about assignments or where they are supposed to rotate. We want them reacting and attacking. We think that's the best way to play defense at this level.

We attack, but we're also constantly reminding them of the importance of not getting beat deep. We are so determined not to give up the deep pass that we tell our free safeties that they have zero run responsibilities. We don't want them worrying about the run and we don't want them getting beat on play-action. Nothing irritates us more than when a free safety bites on a play-action pass. They always think they're responsible for a run up the middle, but we've got six other guys there. Even on a sweep, the free safety's first job is to defend the halfback pass.

Another reason we keep it simple is our scheme has built-in versatility because we employ a hybrid player we call "Spartan" as the weak-side linebacker. We want faster athletes on the perimeter to defend swing passes, screen passes, and sweeps by turning ball carriers inside and into the teeth of our defense. The Spartan has to be one of the best athletes on our team. He has to have good speed, cover skills, an aggressive attitude, and great tackling skills.

The Spartan lines up four yards off the line and two yards outside the last man on the line of scrimmage. Our Mike (middle) and Willie (weak-side) linebackers are inside. Our strong safety is more of an undersized linebacker who lines up as the strong-side outside linebacker and defends against screens and sweeps and tries to turn off-tackle plays inside. We don't want the strong safety running with receivers deep down the field because he's more of a linebacker type, so our Spartan drops back and splits the field with the free safety when we're in Cover-2.

The only downside to our Spartan scheme is he has to be able to handle pulling guards on weak-side power plays, which can be difficult. His primary function on those plays, however, is to get upfield quickly and force the play inside. Our Spartan might be smaller than a typical outside linebacker, but he's also quicker and can therefore hopefully get upfield to disrupt plays more quickly and avoid those blocks.

We don't like receivers running free. We're going to take those guys on and be physical in order to interrupt their routes and make them work to get downfield. That's the bottom line. If receivers are getting off the line clean everywhere, it makes it too hard to defend the entire field. Our defensive backs and linebackers work on rerouting receivers all spring and summer. Nobody gets an easy release. Receivers don't like that. Challenging receivers makes it easier for the cornerbacks to make their reads. It helps the pass rush, too, giving them an extra second to get to the quarterback.

We want our defensive backs physically taking on blocks, shedding blocks, and attacking the ball carrier. Sometimes you see a defensive back stand flat footed and wait for the offensive player to initiate contact. We tell our guys to be the hammer and not the nail. We want everybody attacking and rallying to the ball. If the ball carrier breaks one tackle, we've got another guy coming and another guy coming after that. When we don't see that level of effort in practice, when the cornerback opposite the play is not sprinting to the whistle, for example, we make every defensive player touch the ball carrier on every play.

Goal Line and Prevent

We play a straight man-to-man with an extra defensive lineman when we're in goal line situations. Our inside linebacker takes the running back, the strong safety takes the tight end, and the cornerbacks play the receivers. Our goal is to stop everything up the middle, and if they run outside, we just have to react. If the opposing coach wants to throw on the goal line, he can be my guest.

In the prevent defense, we run a four-deep scheme so the Spartan drops back, meaning both cornerbacks, the Spartan, and the free safety are playing deep. Sometimes we'll replace our Willie linebacker with a nickel back, but I don't like to do that. Teams run a lot of screen passes in this situation, and if you put a bunch of small, fast guys on the field, all of a sudden they have offensive linemen coming at them, and it's a Catch-22. It only works if you're playing man, which isn't a bad idea because it puts a defender on the screen guy right away. If you're going to play prevent, know who they want to hit, what routes they want to run, and whether they have someone they want to bring in specifically for screens. We use a four-man rush so we still get pressure.

‖‖‖

Rugby Tackling

By De La Salle defensive and special teams coordinator Terry Eidson

There will always be concussions in football because there will always be collisions. The game is fast, and players are going to run into each other. However, if everybody learns to tackle with their shoulders and not their heads, I truly believe concussions can be reduced dramatically.

Poor coaching technique has contributed to the problem. Generations of players were taught to plant their facemask in the chest of the ball carrier, which exposes the head to injury. The days when players recklessly smashed into everybody in sight while sacrificing their brains for entertainment have come and gone. Eliminating the head all together is the new direction of the game and rightfully so.

For years we taught De La Salle players to put their facemask on the ball when tackling, but they still had a tendency to use their heads. Then we taught that it should always be the shoulder that strikes with the head to the side. At no point should the head strike the frame of the ball carrier. Then we saw Seattle Seahawks coach Pete Carroll's instructional video on rugby-style tackling during the 2014 offseason. Carroll and Seahawks passing game coordinator Rocky Seto devised an approach to shoulder tackling that can be practiced in shorts and T-shirts. Inspired by rugby players who rely on shoulder tackling, the new philosophy maintains the physical nature of the game while taking the head out of the equation and therefore reducing concussions and other head and neck injuries.

The Seahawks approach has been so effective at the NFL level that Carroll produced a 22-minute video demonstrating various shoulder tackling techniques that was distributed to 14,000 high school and 8,000 youth programs via the video platform Hudl. When Coach

Alumbaugh and I saw the video during the 2014 offseason, it made so much sense that we quickly adopted the new tackling philosophy for the ensuing 2014 season. We drilled it during the spring and summer and told our defensive players to just tackle the ball carrier and quit worrying about big hits. We not only had one of our best tackling seasons in 2014, but for the first time in several years we played a 15-game season without a defensive concussion. This offseason we're going to teach it to our freshman and junior varsity. The following fundamentals were outlined in Carroll's instructional video.

- **TRACKING** describes the defensive player closing the distance with the ball carrier while maintaining leverage. Defenders should track the near-side hip of the ball carrier, adjusting their angle of pursuit when the ball carrier changes path. In the run and gather drill: defenders in a tackling posture with squared shoulders gather themselves while closing on a ball carrier until he can use his shoulder to strike the ball carrier's near hip.

- The **HAWK TACKLE** is a shoulder-leverage tackle where the tackler contacts the ball carrier at the thighs with his right shoulder and squeezes the thighs to his chest. Emphasize eyes through the thighs, wrapping, squeezing, and driving for five steps.

- **HAWK ROLL TACKLE** is the same as the **HAWK TACKLE** with the ball carrier being wrapped up at the thighs except the runner is rolled to the ground. Emphasize eyes through the thighs, wrapping, squeezing, and rolling. This tackle can be practiced using a pad to simulate the outside thigh of the ball carrier.

- The **PROFILE TACKLE** is a shoulder leverage tackle in which the tackler contacts the ball carrier by placing his shoulder on the near breastplate or pec. These tackles are usually made above the waist. Attack the near pec and wrap and drive for five hard steps if the ball carrier does not go down immediately.

- The **STRIKE ZONE** is the area below the neck and above the knees of a defenseless player, much like a baseball strike zone. Contact is made using the shoulder at all times, and therefore neither player's helmet is involved in the play. Tacklers must adjust their aiming point as the receiver lowers his body in anticipation of a hit. This can be practiced by having tacklers attempt to strike a moving chest shield that represents the strike zone.

- **COMPRESSION TACKLES** occur when a combination of players from different position groups apply their fundamental tackling techniques simultaneously and in combination. Both tacklers track the inside hip of the ball carrier and bring their near foot up as they close to striking distance. The front-side defender must turn back the ball carrier, and the back-side defender must close.

CHAPTER 6

Special Teams

How you approach special teams will reflect the identity of your team.

—De La Salle defensive and special

teams coordinator Terry Eidson

Offense sells tickets. Defense wins games. Special teams wins championships. That's what I truly believe. Special teams are a critical part of the game because there aren't a lot of coaches who really pay attention to it. I always felt it was an untapped area. Name a coach who gives equal time to all three phases? All the coaches I've ever known are more worried about getting their offenses and defenses up to speed. For even some of the elite programs in Southern California, it's an afterthought.

Only a select few programs look at special teams as an opportunity to make a huge difference in a game and attack. We attack on offense, we attack on defense, and we attack on special teams, and it has been a huge advantage for us through the years. It can be an advantage for you, too.

Lad lost 25 games during his 34-year career, and in every one of them, there was a special team's gaffe that contributed to it. In my first loss as a high school coach in 1984, for example, the opposing team scored on a fake field goal, and we missed an extra point. A 1987 North Coast Section championship game defeat included a fake punt for a touchdown. In our last loss in 1991 before our 151-game winning streak began, we missed an extra point. The list goes on. If you're honest with yourself and review your toughest losses, you will likely come to the same conclusion.

Special teams creates field position, and field position is critical in high school football because high school kids are more prone to the types of mistakes that prevent long, time-consuming drives. If you can pin an offense deep in its own territory, the odds of the opponent driving 70 or 80 yards are remote. It's the same on offense. As prolific as our offenses have been over the years, when we are scoring 40-plus points per game, it's because we're pinning them deep with our coverage teams, popping big returns, and driving the ball 35 or 40 yards.

Our motto is: offense sells tickets, defense wins games, and special teams wins championships. (Photo by Bob Larson)

Keep this in mind, too: field goal kicking is typically a 50/50 proposition at this level. Touchdowns win games, and, for reasons stated earlier, superior field position translates into more touchdowns.

Passion Is Essential

The best piece of advice I would give a head coach who wants to emphasize special teams is to hire someone who is passionate about it. I was an average high school football player. Special teams were the one thing I was decent at, and I thought it was a lot of fun. At 5'10", 145 pounds, I could block punts, field goals, and extra points. I remember our high school special teams coach said he would shave his head if we ever caused a fumble. During one game we not only caused a fumble but recovered it, but he refused to shave. He motivated us to be good on special teams, even though he didn't follow through. I was furious. I knew I wanted to coach special teams even then. I remember thinking, *I'm never going to be that guy. I'm going to follow through.*

I was real interested in special teams when I was the junior varsity coach at De La Salle. Our special teams back then were nothing special. The returns were blasé. When Lad brought me up to the varsity, I wanted something that was mine. I wanted special teams to be my responsibility. Lad said, "You can have it." He hasn't asked me a question about special teams since.

Not long after, we made it our goal that we wanted to win a game without a touchdown on offense or defense. We wanted to win a game with special teams. We didn't want to just get the ball back. We wanted to score. I knew if I could get guys to buy in we could start scoring. Then it started happening. I told one of our returners before the season that if he scored I would shave my beard. He scored in the first game, and I shaved without hesitation. My wife Aggie took one look at me when I got home and said: "How long before that grows back?"

A coach has to be passionate about it to make his players passionate about it, pure and simple.

Create a Physical Identity

Special teams can create an aggressive identity for your team because you have to be fast and physical to play great special teams. Start a game with 10 mad men sprinting down the field on the kickoff team, fighting off blocks, and rallying to the ball. That sets the tone. If you get a big hit, not only does it impact the crowd, but your sideline also goes crazy, your defense is fired up running onto the field, and the other team slinks off, deflated. It's the same if you spring a big return. We often have guys blocking three or four guys on the same play on our big returns. The tone is set. Our attitude has been established. We're going to hit you and block you all over the field for the entire game. That's the message we're looking to send. Offensive and defensive players see the special teams guys flying around and giving maximum effort and are inspired to do the same.

In our 2014 season opener, we played against one of the top teams in Northern California, Jesuit-Carmichael High, who just so happened to be coached by Marlon Blanton, one of our former players. I didn't think he was going to kick to us so I just had a generic return called. We scored on the opening kickoff. Our kickoff team pinned them deep, and then we blocked a punt despite having only 10 men on the field. We recovered at the 2-yard line and scored on the next play, and the game was essentially over and we'd only run one offensive play for two yards. That's the power of special teams.

Big plays on special teams are always huge momentum plays because they usually involve a big hit, a long return, or a drastic change in field position. Then you have to make sure you keep playing good special teams, or the momentum could go the other way. In a 2014 game against South Carolina power Byrnes High School, for example, we threw a short pass on a fake punt and scored on a 65-yard play. It was a huge momentum builder against a nationally ranked opponent. Then what did we do? We gave up the ensuing kick return for a touchdown and gave the momentum away.

Part of Our DNA

I love it when I hear or read about coaches who tell their teams that they're playing De La Salle this week and therefore they need to take special teams seriously because in my mind those teams are already beat. You can't fake it. It's like discipline. You can't say you're going to be disciplined this week. You have to be disciplined *every* week. You can't emphasize it one week and not the next. Like being disciplined, special teams have to be part of your team's DNA.

If you are aggressive and physical on special teams, you will have an aggressive, physical team. If you are lazy on special teams, you will have a lazy team. If you try to rest guys on special teams, you're telling them they can take plays off on offense and defense, too. That's the message you're sending. How you approach special teams will reflect the identity of your team.

If you asked our kids if they think Coach Eidson takes special teams seriously, they would say, "Are you kidding me?" Everything I do, every scouting report, every film session, every T-shirt I give out, every practice, every pregame meeting emphasizes how important it is to me. When they come in on Monday, I tell them how we're going to block a punt. I have them watch film of the opposing team's kickoff returns. When they come to practice on Tuesday, the punt block is on the board along with their kickoff return schemes. I look for a weakness in the opposing team's special teams that we can exploit. I explain it to the kids, and they get excited about it. It's part of what we do, as big a part of our scouting report and gameplan as our offense and defense. Players are required to know their assignments on offense, defense, *and* special teams. I don't tell them it's important. They *know* it's important because I emphasize it every day. If they don't take it seriously or if they are nonchalant out there or are using special teams to take a break from offense or defense, they're gone. Good-bye. I don't hesitate. Then the player will find himself sitting on the bench thinking to himself: *Okay, I get it. I'm sorry. I understand how important it is. I won't do that again.* As a coach, you can't just give it lip service.

Best Players Play

If you use second and third-string guys on special teams and you kick off to us, you're in trouble. We're going to have our starting linemen out there. That's going to be a huge advantage for us. We don't hide players on special teams or play backup players just to get them in the game. If you do that, you're telling your team that special teams don't matter. You don't put second and third-string players on offense or defense, so why would you put them on special teams?

We play our best players on special teams. The only exception is we typically don't use guys who are already playing both offense and defense. If it's a toss-up, we try to use the kid who doesn't play on offense or defense, but they have to prove they are an asset. I make it abundantly clear to our players that even if they don't start on offense or defense, they can still make a significant contribution as a special teams player. Kids know and respect that. Virtually every kid on the team thinks he's going to be a starter heading into the season. Kids are optimistic that way. If they don't nail down that starting offensive or defensive position, they need to know they can still make a *huge* impact by playing special teams.

If they are fast enough, we might use a backup offensive or defensive lineman on our return teams because we want our fastest linemen to set up the wall. Our kids know and our fans know that if our returner catches the ball and gets a few steps going, some big blocks are coming. Sometimes players on teams that have played us for years understand what's about to happen and they'll either stop or do everything they can to avoid contact. Everybody's head is on swivel. Those kids have seen us on film and they're thinking, *Uh, oh.*

That's why I think a coach should have an obligation to emphasize special teams because sometimes kids see us on film and know they don't want any part of us. They realize they have not been put in a position to succeed. They don't want to get clobbered so they don't go full speed, which is a huge advantage for us as well. Sometimes the opposing coverage team is surprised when we run a specific return. That means the staff hasn't scouted us at all. Those kids don't know what's coming. This isn't going to end well. You're not doing a third-string kid any favors by trotting him out there against a team that takes special teams as seriously as we do. When we do run into a team that emphasizes special teams, which doesn't happen often, and they've got good gunners trying to interrupt our returns, they can cause us some problems, too, no doubt about it.

Sometimes starting players don't want to play special teams. That's very unusual at De La Salle. More often, I've got two or three starters in my ear trying to get out there. We've emphasized it to a point where it's a real honor to be a member of those teams and even the two-way starters are begging to get out there.

We don't rest kids on special teams either. If a running back breaks an 80-yard run and he also happens to be on the kickoff team, we might put someone else in so he can get a breather. But we don't do that very often. We condition the kids with that in mind, too. They need to understand that even if they were playing guard on a 12-play drive that they need to be out there on the ensuing kickoff because the next play is just as important as any of the plays on the previous drive.

A lot of the time, my special teams captain or seniors will suggest someone they think should either be on a team or off of it. They might say, "Put Chris on the kickoff team. That guy is tough," or "Take Reid off the kickoff return team. He doesn't want to be out there." I listen to the kids and usually act accordingly.

Application Required

Once you find a coach who is passionate about special teams, you have to find players equally passionate. You only want guys playing special teams who want to do it. If you have to convince them or beg them, it won't work. I take it a step further. The only way you can play special teams for me is if you fill out an application.

There are no exceptions. Sometimes a player won't fill one out at the beginning of the season and will decide later he wants to try. I still make him fill out an application. If a couple guys get hurt and you need to bring somebody up, they have to fill out an application to be considered.

Here is my special teams application form:

Special teams are an extremely important part of the game of football. Games are decided by great or poor special teams play. We will not win a championship unless we play great special teams. Great special teams

play is a SPARTAN tradition and the question is are you
up for that challenge?

Former New York Jets coach Walt Michaels summed up what
kind of man plays special teams: "A man with no fear
belongs in two places — a mental institution and on
special teams." **ARE YOU THAT MAN?**

1. What special teams are you applying for?

2. What are your goals for each team you are applying
   for?

3. How do you plan on making these goals a reality?

4. Why should I put you on special teams?

A separate application for the kickoff team follows:

1. What have you done to be worthy of this team?

2. What are your serious, realistic goals for this
   very special team?

3. Explain how important the kickoff team is to the
   game of football and your life.

4. When have you experienced the most pain?

5. What movie best describes your attitude for
   kickoffs? Be specific.

6. What would you do if you saw your mother running
   with a football?

The last question came from an article I read on special teams years ago. If the response is "push her out of bounds," the player is best suited for offense. If it's "tackle her," he's a defensive player. If they write "knock her head off," then you know for sure you have a quality special teams candidate.

Players have gone to great lengths when filling out their applications. D.J. Williams, who went on to play for the Miami Hurricanes, Denver Broncos, and Chicago Bears, included a video of him tackling his mother, who was dressed in pads and a De La Salle uniform. I quickly put an end to that. Over the years kids have submitted video of themselves running through grocery stores, slamming into each other while holding rubber playground balls, or jumping out of moving vehicles. I finally had to put an end to videos for obvious reasons.

Sometimes a kid will prick his finger and smear blood all over the application, which is always good for a laugh. One kid grew up racing motocross and wrote about how he flipped his bike, broke three ribs, and had to walk half a mile. I said, "Now, *that's* what we're looking for."

It's Not About Schemes

I won't introduce special teams schemes here because they don't matter. On special teams, it's never about schemes. It's about *effort*. If people think we have good special teams schemes, it's only because our guys hustle and make it a good scheme. There's something to getting set up and being organized, sure, but there are a million ways to cover and return if kids are willing to make blocks and tackles. When something goes wrong on special teams, it's always became of a lack of effort somewhere. It's not because somebody outschemed us.

If we mash a defense all the way down the field and score a touchdown and then the PAT gets blocked because a defender gets through untouched, it's not the result of a brilliant scheme but a lineman who decided to rest.

Our punt team has gotten more diverse through the years and added more formations (more on that later). We've run the exact same kickoff return for 25 years, and it still works. Everybody knows the scheme. You would have to be an idiot not to know what we're going to do. Every kid on both sides knows what's coming, and it still works. Why? It's pretty simple. Who wants it more?

Their guys run down, see our guys coming at them, and slow up or try not to get blocked, and it opens up huge holes. It works every time. Our first-team kickoff team hadn't given up a return for a touchdown since I took over special teams duties in 1991. In 2014 when we finished No. 1 in the state and No. 2 in the nation, we gave up two. We didn't change our scheme, that's for sure.

One of the first things people notice after seeing De La Salle play for the first time is our effort. It's a wonderful compliment—probably the best one a coach could ever receive. We create that effort with our weight training, with our conditioning, and with our commitment to one another. It has been engrained through the years and is the signature of our program.

That said, I still don't know how realistic it is for offensive and defensive players to go all-out on every play—no matter how much we emphasize it as coaches—when they are playing 60 or 70 plays a game. If you're the left tackle and the ball is being run to the right side, it's human nature to take a play off here and there. It's the same on defense, though, you obviously want to minimize that as much as possible

On special teams, however, there's absolutely no reason to take a play off or to give anything less than full-out, 100 percent effort. It's one play! If you're only going to be out there for one play, there's no reason not to go full bore. We find 11 guys who will do that. If someone's not hustling or is taking a play off, there's always somebody willing to get in there and go 100 percent.

Create a Culture

Years ago I got all the special teams guys together, and we watched *Walking Tall*, the Joe Don Baker movie about the small town sheriff who single-handedly cleans up his corrupt community using nothing more than a four-foot hickory club. It was a great bonding moment. I loved those kids, and they loved each other.

When *Ghostbusters* came out, we were playing our rival, and one of our best players said: "Who you gonna call? Wedgebusters!" A couple years after that, another player had vanity license plates made that read: "Busters 85." It took off from there. Ever since our kickoff team has been called "Busters." Even if we win 100–0, if we give up any kind of return, my phone blows up with texts and calls from outraged former Busters.

The culture just kind of evolved through the years. The details don't matter. What does is that you find a way to make special teams fun. A head coach can't necessarily do that. It needs to be an assistant in my opinion. If the head coach screws around too much, sometimes the kids take it the wrong way, as if it's okay for them to screw around, too.

The point is that every program should incorporate something to lighten things up and allow the kids to have fun. It should be something that fires them up and gets them going, something that will be a memory for them, however you go about it. You can't just keep hammering kids about being good at special teams. There has to be a reward, something that appeals to boys that age. Whatever you're going to do, it has to be something you would do in front of your mother, even if she might roll her eyes. Be careful not to get too personal with kids. You always have to watch what you say to kids. They take things literally. Never use insults. It's easy to get carried away. Don't let that happen.

We get the special teams applicants together at the start of every season and watch a movie that emphasizes guts, determination, and courage. Former players often send me recommendations. One year we watched the Sylvester Stallone movie, *Cobra*. The kids loved it. One of them bought *Cobra* sunglasses at a toy store. I put them on, and they started chanting "Cobra, Cobra." It's continued to build through the years until I now wear a black leather jacket, black pants, and boots. Several years ago my wife dared me to get a "Cobra" tattoo on my bicep. Of course I did. I give out a "Cobra Corps" T-shirt with an iconic quote from that year's movie on the back. Kids will do anything for one of those T-shirts.

Cobra makes its first appearance on the Thursday before the first game when I announce the special teams captain, which everybody

The Cobra Corps unit of De La Salle not only displays the pride we take in our special teams play, but also shows the importance of developing a fun culture to engage the guys. (Yary Sports Photography, Northern California)

understands is just as important as the offensive and defensive captains. The special teams captain receives the first Cobra Corps T-shirt for that season. The captain then gets to wear my leather jacket during practice, which is hilarious because, though it's only a run-through, it's usually 90 degrees that early in the season, and he ends up sweating like crazy.

Cobra appears from time to time, but only when quality special teams play warrants it. I put on the garb and read media stories about people doing heroic things. "Man Shot Three Times Drives Self Home" is an old favorite. Overcoming pain is an ongoing theme. When Aron Ralston, the person portrayed by James Franco in *127 Hours*, amputated his arm with a dull knife to free himself from a dislodged boulder after being trapped for five days, I knew I had another classic.

The kickoff team gets together and plays a song before every game. That's another tradition. They can pick out any song they think will fire them up as long as it's appropriate and doesn't contain f-bombs.

At the end of the year, our players vote on the Special Teams Player of the Year, which we award at our team banquet. Once that tradition was established, that honor is considered by our players as prestigious as any of our awards.

I don't know if Cobra makes us play better special teams or not, but the kids seem to have fun with it and so do I. It's a device that helps me convince them that special teams are special. In 2014 the backup special teams players took their roll so seriously they would get together on their own to study the other teams' schemes to give the starters the best possible look during practice.

A couple years ago, I started to wonder if Cobra had run its course, and maybe it was time for him to retire. I pulled a couple of my core guys aside and asked them for their honest opinion. *Hey, I do this for the kids. It wasn't going to hurt my feelings if they thought it was time to try something else.* Instead, they said: "Are you kidding, me? We love it!" So Cobra lives on.

Practicing Special Teams

I used to start practice with special teams, especially on Thursdays, because I wanted to emphasize it and let the kids know how important it was. The problem was our school is so academically oriented that kids often have to be tutored after school, and they miss the beginning of practice. It was the same thing when kids needed extra therapy in the training room. I would be missing a third of my guys, and the kids who didn't play special teams would stretch and warm up and then they would have to wait around for us to finish, which was a lousy way for them to start practice. It was driving me crazy, so a few years ago, we started incorporating special teams into our normal practice schedule.

Now, I wouldn't do it any other way.

If we're working with the offense, I might yell "punt team" after a play, and the punt team runs onto the field just like it would in a game, and we'll practice that. If we're starting to wrap up the defensive part of practice, I might yell "punt return team," and they hustle onto the field to simulate a game situation. We also work our kickoff return, kickoff, PAT, and field goal teams into the normal flow of practice, and it works extremely well for a couple of reasons.

Let's say the offense is struggling to run a play properly. Frustration is building. I call "punt team," and an offensive coach can carry over a coaching point and work with those players while waiting for us to finish. Then they can go back and apply what they've learned. There's less standing around that way.

I always like to wait until we've been in pads for a couple days before I start assembling special teams units because I want to see these guys hit first. You will always have a pretty good idea about who your returners are going to be, but I need to see everybody else in pads to find out who our hitters are.

Then a week or two into fall practice, I will have the punt team stay after practice one day, the punt return team the next. I keep each team after practice for a half hour, and we walk through our schemes and the players' responsibilities and then we practice them again during normal practice the following day.

I always save the first live kickoff team practice for the first Saturday scrimmage because that's our most prestigious special team.

During a normal week, if we're working on offense on Tuesday, for example, we'll work the punt, field goal, and PAT teams. If Tuesday's practice is defensive-oriented, we will work on punt return and kickoff return. On Thursdays I work on kickoff, onside kick, and taking a safety with our punt team. I probably spend 10 to 15 minutes a day on special teams, which adds up to about an hour and 10 minutes for the week.

You never want anything to happen in a game that you haven't practiced so I try to go over every conceivable scenario during the week. It's 17–14, seven seconds left, fourth down, 7-yard line. We don't want to risk a punt block or a fair catch and a free catch, so we need to take a safety to run out the clock. We practice that. We haven't had that situation unfold in 15 years, but we practice it.

There is a little known free kick rule. The rule is: if a game or half ends with a punt, and the return man calls for a fair catch and if the ball doesn't hit the ground, the returner can hand the ball to the official and ask for a free kick even if the clock has expired. The receiving team can then attempt a field goal. I've been waiting for that situation to arise for my entire career. When we finally got a chance in 2014, the kids were prepared and we just missed a 48-yarder.

Sometimes an assistant coach will suggest we do something we haven't practiced. The answer is always no. Unless we've practiced it, we won't do it in a game.

‖‖‖

Punting

By De La Salle secondary and special teams/kicking coach Donnie Boyce

I just look for someone who doesn't look stiff and has a good foot and I go from there. I show them how to punt in two steps because they not only need to be able to punt the ball, but they also need to do it quickly. They should be in a staggered stance with the left foot slightly forward when they receive the snap.

A right-footed punter should then take a longer momentum step with his right foot before setting the plant foot, standing tall, and kicking through the laces on top of the ball with the goal of achieving a minimum hang time of four seconds.

When they catch the snap, I want them holding the back end or the cone with the fingertips of their right hand. It shouldn't be sucked into their palm. The left hand is a guide hand that secures the cone of the ball to the fingertips on the right hand. The right arm should be at handshake level extended with the right elbow slightly bent. The ball itself should be at approximately a 20-degree angle when it is dropped on the right hip with the laces on top. Holding the ball with the fingertips of the right hand helps make for a consistent drop. Before releasing the ball, the punter should allow himself to momentarily guide the ball in a downward motion to ensure it drops straight down and is as flat as possible. It should not spin or fall end over end. If he's trying a directional kick to the right or left, he should step to the right or left, but the ball should still be dropped on the right hip for a right-footed punter and on the left hip for a left-footer.

I tell our punters to lock their kicking foot in an outstretched position and then attempt to kick the ball through the laces to encourage the proper follow-through. Punters always want to kick a spiral and they try to spin the ball off the side of their outstretched foot, but that's not how you kick a spiral. If he drops the ball flat and at a 45-degree angle, he has increased his odds of hitting the sweet spot. Hitting the sweet spot and driving the ball straight up through the laces causes the ball to roll off the foot, and they will get the spiral they're looking for.

Here are the two most common mistakes I see our punters make. 1) They push the ball too far in front of them before dropping it and end up kicking the back of the ball, and it goes end over end. 2) They drop the ball not on the hip but in the middle of their bodies, forcing them to swing their kicking leg to the right or left to center the foot under the ball. That's how shanks occur.

I have our punters practice their angle kicks and our quarterbacks practice pooch kicks. We often line up in our split-back veer offense with the quarterback in the shotgun on fourth down to prevent the other team from bringing their punt return team onto the field. The quarterback begins his cadence with "Down!" before taking two steps backward and setting himself again. Then he continues his cadence with "Set!...Hut!" When he receives the snap, he makes a one-step kick with the goal of punting the ball 20 to 25 yards down the field and over the safety's head where hopefully he will get a good roll.

I always tell my kicker to practice punting, too, because if my punter starts at another position I don't want him punting and risking injury in a lopsided game.

For drills we have our punters go through dry runs. We have them put the ball in one hand, spin it, and then catch it as if receiving the snap. Set the ball at the proper position on the hip. They are then to proceed with their steps without dropping the ball before swinging the leg as if punting the ball at half speed with an exaggerated follow-through.

We practice the drop by having them take their steps and dropping the ball, but we don't want them swinging their leg at all. The goal is to land the ball so flat on the grass that it bounces straight up in the air.

We have them do this back and forth across the field approximately 50 to 100 times.

Punters should compete against each other to see how many kicks they can get inside the 10-yard line. They should also compete for hang time, distance, and the time it takes for the punter to receive the snap and punt the ball, which should take no more than 2.4 seconds.

I have noticed that a lot of punters look lost when an opponent breaks a punt return and they are the last person available to make the tackle. I remedy this by having our punters kick to a returner and then pursue him down the field not to make a big hit necessarily but to help the punter learn the angles required to prevent a returner from running full speed for the entire length of the field.

Punt Team

This is the unit we spend the most time with and the unit that has evolved the most through my years as special teams coach. My primary goal with the punt team is to put the opposition into defensive mode. I want to make them so glad to get the ball back that they don't even attempt a return. I don't even want to give them a chance to get their punt return team on the field.

We have a tight formation, which is basically seven men on the line, two wings, a protector, and a punter. From there we shift into a wider formation we call "Hokie" because Virginia Tech started doing this years ago. We spread out a little wider with everybody spreading about three steps. We can also go even wider where we spread out the formation from hash to hash.

Then we have what we call a "lightning" formation, which works best on fourth and 6 or fourth and 7. We will keep our offense on the field so opposing coaches are forced to keep their defense out there. (It doesn't hurt that we go for it so often on fourth down that opposing teams are always wary of us going for it.) We let the officials spot the ball, and then I will yell "Hokie lightning," and our punt team will sprint onto the field while the offense sprints off. The punt team sets up quickly, and we punt it. We end up with a lot of 12-men-on-the-field penalties if the opposing team tries to rush either their punt return team or a returner onto the field. If it doesn't, we've succeeded in keeping its defense on the field, at least. If we can make our opponents adjust to what we're doing, we've won the battle.

Opposing teams know we're going to do it and spend a lot of time practicing against it, which works to our advantage, too. A lot of the time, it turns into paralysis by analysis, and they will be so worried about not making a mistake that they make mistakes.

Sometime we just line the offense up in a shotgun formation and have the quarterback punt it. That also keeps the return team off the field. In 2014 we had a good field goal kicker, but on fourth and 20, I wasn't confident he could kick a 47-yarder, so we snapped directly to him in field-goal formation, and he dinked it down inside the 20-yard line.

We frequently run our lightning team onto the field at the last minute and then go on a hard count, which can draw the opponents offside. It has become a signature play and one that drives opposing coaches crazy. In 2013 we were playing Southern California powerhouse Servite High and had a fourth and 12 near midfield. We ran our lightning punt team on the field and caught them with a 12th man, making it fourth and 7. Then we ran the lightning team out again but went on a long count and drew them offside, making it fourth and 2. Then we ran our regular offense out at the last minute, lined up, and got the first down. I call that the trifecta. Opponents know it's coming, have prepared for it all week, and still fall victim to it. Our kids love it.

We've got an offside play we run with our field goal team, too, but since we usually have a good kicker, I only use it when we really need a touchdown. I also have a couple trick field goal plays we can use.

» KICKING

We take a different approach to kicking for a couple reasons. First, our offense is so prolific that we score a lot of touchdowns, which means we have to kick more extra points and kick the ball off more than most teams. Secondly, our coaching staff is so aggressive that we usually go for it in typical field-goal situations, even if we have a quality field goal kicker, which we usually do.

We might kick five field goals in a season and close to 100 extra points and kickoffs, so we concentrate on finding kicking candidates who can consistently put the ball in the end zone when kicking off and can routinely make extra points and short field goals.

It's rare for a kicker to have had much coaching before he arrives on our campus as a freshman, so we look for kids who can naturally kick the ball and work from there. It's not that much different from identifying a kid who can naturally swing a baseball bat or a golf club. Some kids just have a knack.

I like to watch a kid kick for a while to gauge his natural abilities, and then we start working on the best way to hit the sweet spot consistently. Kicking is a lot like a golf swing. There are a lot of different ways to do it successfully. There are a lot of things I could teach them so they would kick it the way I would kick it or the way NFL kickers, whose form is flawless, kick it, but not everybody can do what I can do or what NFL kickers can do. Therefore, those coaching points may not work best for them.

All soccer-style approaches look similar, but there are little things a coach can change to help them be more consistent. Kids always want to kick it to the moon, for example. But again to use the golf analogy, a player typically hits his longest drives when he's not trying to kill it but hit it squarely and on the sweet spot. The foot has a sweet spot just like a golf club and a baseball bat. If you can keep the approach consistent, you can get a kid with a knack for kicking and a willingness to practice and be coached to consistently hit 40-yard field goals.

Our kickers do a lot of stretching. We have them do lunges for 50 yards for stretching and strengthening purposes. Then we have them pick a yard line, take two sidesteps, and practice their field goal steps with their foot swinging straight down the yard line. We have them do that at about 50 percent of normal velocity from sideline to sideline with an exaggerated follow-through.

» KICKOFFS

I typically like my kickers seven to 10 yards from the ball on kickoffs. The approach creates a buildup of momentum that allows the kicker to gain more depth. It should be as straight as possible, and the kicker should approach the spot where the plant foot will land and not the ball. That way he will have his plant foot down and can extend his kicking foot through the ball.

If a kicker lines up at less than seven yards, they usually end up rushing to get the necessary momentum. The key is having the foot farther away from the ball than you would on a field goal because the momentum is going through the ball and not stopping on a plant foot like it would on a field goal. We don't want anything other than the kicker's non-kicking big toe to touch the yard line before the ball is kicked. On a kickoff the plant foot is more like the first step of a triple jump. You're rolling through the ball. We want our kicker to build his momentum, explode through the ball, and finish with a little crow hop as their momentum continues down the field.

All our kickers keep a piece of athletic tape or a bean bag with them to use as a marker for where to begin their approach. On a kickoff, for example, he might march eight steps behind the ball and two to the side. If that's his routine, I want him to put the piece of tape on that spot before he does his dry runs. That way, if he feels like he needs a stutter step, is too compact, or something doesn't feel right, he can adjust piece of tape as necessary. If he notices on his dry run that his foot touches the yard line, he should move the tape back.

I still want my kickers to march off their steps before every dry run, but the tape should remain on the ground. I don't want them to look at the tape when they march off their steps, but it should be directly under them when they have finished to ensure that they're in the right spot. They need to be in that spot every time to be consistent.

During the summer we do 10 to 12 kickoffs three times a week. Once we get into the season, I start limiting their kicking a lot more. As soon as a kicker feels like he's hitting the ball but no longer hitting it hard, he should stop for the day. If you have a kicker kick 15 kickoffs every day in two weeks, he won't be able to reach the 10-yard line, and his leg will be constantly sore, and then you're in trouble.

I might have them kick five kickoffs on a Monday during the season. On Tuesday they can kick three or four if they have something to work on. On Wednesday they kick off when we practice with the kickoff team and they get two or three more reps. On Thursday we have them kick with our kickoff scout team, but we don't want them trying as hard and kicking it out of the end zone because we want our kickoff return team to practice returning it.

If a kicker can consistently kick the ball into the end zone, there's no reason to get fancy. In California and most other states, any ball kicked into the end zone cannot be returned, and the ball is brought out to the 20-yard line. If a kicker struggles to consistently reach the end zone— and for various other game situations—every kicker should also have a pooch, a squib, and an onside kick in his arsenal.

Pooch

A pooch kick is a high, short kick that lands near the numbers on either side of the field between the 20 and 30-yard lines and usually results in the ball being recovered after it hits the ground or a fair catch. It's a safe kick as long as the kicker keeps it in bounds. We tell our kickers to aim for the numbers on either side of the field, so there is room for error.

The pooch kick prevents the opposing team's kick returners from returning the ball. It's also an effective strategy if the wind is blowing in the kicker's face, in which case the wind would likely hold the ball in the air, allowing your coverage team more time to get downfield to cover the kick and prevent a return.

If the ball is to be pooched to the right, we tell our kickers to start their run up to the ball normally but to not gain as much momentum. As they get to within four yards, we want them to begin looping their approach to compensate for the angled kick. This kick requires 25 percent less effort than a normal kickoff. We tell our kickers not to run through the ball the way they would normally but to plant their non-kicking leg like a field goal, which creates a higher trajectory.

Squib

For squib kicks I tell our kickers to try to hit the player directly in front of them in the chest. That player is typically a lineman responsible for setting up a wall on the return, and they rarely step in front of the ball. More often they try to get out of the way. If the kick were to bounce off his chest, it would likely make for an easy recovery by the kicking team.

The ball eventually hits the ground and bounces every which way, making it that much more difficult to return and allowing the clock to drain. The return team is often resigned to jumping on it instead of attempting to return it. It's virtually impossible to set up a return on a squib kick because nobody knows where the ball is going to go. It's a solid strategy if you want to prevent the returner from making an easy basket catch and you want to give your team a chance to recover. It can be especially effective in wet weather when the ball is slippery and in extremely windy conditions. It can also be effective at the end of a game or half when you don't want to pooch it because a fair catch would leave time on the clock for a final play and you don't want to kick it deep to a dangerous return man.

I tell our kickers to strike the middle of the ball at about 80 percent of a normal kickoff when executing a squib kick. On a regular kickoff, I don't want the non-kicking leg to touch the yard line. On a squib kick, that foot should land on the line. We also want the kicker to strike the ball hard to create maximum velocity.

Onside

I can't recall us attempting an onside kick in the decade I've been an assistant coach, but we did unintentionally kick one last year. Since we were up 45–0 at the time, we almost got booed out of the stadium. We told our kicker to pooch it, and he kicked the tee instead of the ball, and it only went about 14 yards and we recovered. We made our kicker go to the opposing coach after the game to apologize and explain what happened.

I tell my kickers to lean the ball against the tee—not on it—and then kick the upper half of the ball instead of the lower half to get it spinning end over end quickly to better create a high bounce. If the ball is teed up normally, muscle memory sometimes kicks in, and the ball gets kicked deep. An onside kick is performed best at half-speed, and success is often the product of hours of trial and error, as it is with the pooch and squib.

Kickers have gotten so efficient at getting the high hop with onside kicks that it's now legal to fair catch an onside kick in California. I think it's a good rule because it prevents a defenseless player from getting creamed while trying to field the ball.

Kickoff Team

Your kickoff team is the heart and soul of your special teams. It takes guts to be on the kickoff team. It's a very high speed play and so much can go wrong. You're sprinting down the field, fighting through blocks. At our level they are trying to limit concussions and rightfully so. I agree with that, but the kickoff team is still a rock 'em, sock 'em part of the game, which is why you have to be really careful when you practice it. You don't want to expose kids to too many hits. For that reason we don't let the kickoff team go live until the first scrimmage because the risk of injury is too severe. It doesn't affect our performance because we run through it without contact so frequently, and the kids are so hyped that when we do go live they are champing at the bit and usually execute real well.

One issue we've run into through the years is we score so much that our kickoff team gets way too many reps. In 2014, for example, we scored 86 touchdowns and kicked four field goals. In all we had 121 kickoffs and only 39 touchbacks. At one point we had 31 straight kickoffs without a touchback, which became a huge concern because my No. 1 concern is protecting kids. We never let a player join the team who hasn't been through the offseason conditioning program. It is a safety issue. There has never been an exception until 2014, when I let a soccer player join the team to be our kickoff specialist only because he could consistently put the ball in the end zone.

» PAT/FIELD GOALS

When kickers step back and to the side to mark off their approach to the ball, they often think they need four steps to kick a 40-yard field goal, but more often their strides end up being too long. They either pull the ball or overcompensate and push it to the right and therefore struggle with consistency. I tell them that the goal of the approach is to gain a little momentum. Keep the approach shorter and more compact, and they won't be lunging after the ball. It should be a simple three-step process.

One step, two steps, plant, kick. Simple.

We start the season practicing our field goal steps (using a piece of tape or a bean bag) until the kickers are comfortably and consistently kicking a stationary ball. Then we introduce the snapper and the holder. That's when it gets challenging. The ball is not always in the same place and can move a couple inches, and that can make all the difference.

We want the ball off in between 1.3 and 1.6 seconds because the kids who line up on the edge and try to block a field goal are usually kids who can run between a 4.4 to 4.7 second 40-yard dash, and they can get to the ball if a snap, hold, and kick takes more than 1.7. We spend a lot of time getting our timing down.

When the kickers are comfortable and consistently accurate with the timing of the snap, I start trying to distract them. I might throw a pad near them when they're kicking to make them maintain their focus. When they get comfortable with that, we line up and go live. Even then, we don't go all-out rush our kickers because we've had accidents where we've run into him when he's in a defenseless position and we don't want to take that risk.

Our kickers might kick 20 to 25 field goals and PATs on a Monday during the season, with only two being from long range. We might have them do 10 to 15 from various places on the field on Tuesday. They might kick five more on Wednesday if they need to work on something. We have them kick with the field goal/PAT teams on Thursday, which is when we try to heap as much pressure as possible on them.

We encourage players and coaches to heckle our kickers when they are attempting field goals in practice because it prepares them for pressure-packed moments they might face during the season. It helps them build the mental toughness that can allow them to run onto the field with the crowd going crazy and kick a game-winner with a couple seconds left on the clock.

We don't let the kids say anything too crazy, of course, and nothing personal. But they might yell "Hook! Hook!" I might tell the kicker that if he misses a field goal the entire team has to run a gasser to put some pressure on him. "C'mon, you *have* to hit this!" Of course, the entire team is cheering. Coach Eidson has even been known to pull cash out of his pocket and make fake bets with other coaches on whether our kicker will make or miss a long field goal.

If you never test your kicker's mental capacity, you're doing him a disservice. Coach Eidson is really good at that. But sometimes you also have to keep a close eye on a kid's demeanor. You don't want him taking anything too personally. Sometimes it's better to leave him alone for a couple days.

Snappers

It's easier to find kickers than snappers. Actually, finding someone to snap for field goals and extra points isn't as difficult because it's a shorter snap. Finding someone who can long snap 14 yards for punts is tougher because the long snapper has to use his legs and arms as he thrusts the ball deep between his legs. Sometimes we use one guy for field goals and another for punts.

I always like to have multiple snappers because I don't want a starting offensive or defensive lineman snapping a football when we're up 35 or 40 points because there is a risk of injury whenever you cover a kick or punt. The problem is it's hard to find one good long snapper, let alone two, so sometimes we put our quarterback in shotgun formation and just have him pooch punt the ball, which, when performed correctly, can be as effective as a punt.

» RETURN TEAMS

If you kick off or punt to us, we're going to score. That's our attitude. Our schemes are not designed to just get the ball back or fair catch or play it safe. We've got our best returners out there. Our return teams are an extension of our offense, and our offense attacks. We use our fastest linemen to set up walls. Even on our back wedge, we don't want a 320-pounder back there. We want somebody who can run. On punt return they have to be big enough to hold their own in case of a fake, of course, but what we're looking for is speed so we can set up our walls quickly. If a guy can't run, the return doesn't work.

On the punt return team, we put our best man-to-man defenders on the opposing team's gunners. The inside linebacker picks up anybody who slips through. We use two returners and tell the secondary returner, or the one not catching the ball, that he can't worry about a possible fumble. The secondary returner's instinct is to make sure the primary returner catches the ball, but that's not his responsibility. He has to take that for granted because his primary job is to protect the primary returner and to therefore making the catch easier. He does this by running over and telling the primary returner how much time he has before the coverage team converges and/or whether or not to fair catch. Then his job is to attack the first threat to the primary returner. The primary and secondary returners have a unique relationship in our scheme, and the only way to get them comfortable is to practice it.

Because of our attacking attitude, I understand that we're going to get some clips throughout the season. It's going to happen. When our punt return guys peel back, there's always a chance of a clip. Kids are kids. They get excited. They see a big play coming, and it happens. We live with it. That's just how we play.

The first goal is to end up in the end zone. The secondary goal for our return teams is to average 15 to 20 yards per punt return and for our kick return team to return the ball to our 40-yard line.

Blocking Punts and Kickoffs

Like everybody else I look for weak spots on the opposing punt team. We watch how the other teams rush them and how they block and where there might be an opening. Does the center leaving early create a hole in the middle? Sometimes you can go over a guy or find a way to create a hole. The reason we don't block more punts is we get so far ahead. If we're up 21–0, for example, I don't want to risk a momentum change by roughing the punter. If things are going our way, I don't like to give teams an opportunity to get back in the game.

It's virtually impossible to block a PAT if the other team has a good snapper unless you go straight up the middle, and that's dangerous to practice because somebody is bound to get nailed. The kids always want to try to block PATs. I tell them, "No, let's let them show us how we're going to block their field goal later in the game." That way, if you need to block a field goal in a close game you know where to go.

Trick Plays

When I was the junior varsity coach, I started every game with a trick play. That probably sounds crazy, but the kids loved it and so did I. It's important to do things that add excitement and fun to the program. It's fun to run around, go quickly, and draw a team offside. On the sideline everybody is fired up. We obviously don't run trick plays if the score is lopsided because we don't want to humiliate the other team, but sometimes I'll run one late in the season because I want to throw a bone to a hardworking special teams player. The kids are always begging me to let them try the fake field goal or whatever. If I do run a trick play when we don't need it, it's to set another trick play up for a bigger game later in the year.

The head coach should know about any trick play you run. Don't take that for granted. Lad would always watch us practice a trick play and then dismiss it. "That will never work," he would say, waving his hand in mocking fashion. "It's too slow developing." But even he would have to admit that we have pulled off a lot of successful trick plays on special teams over the years.

We were working on a fake punt heading into a game televised by ESPN in 2014. I asked Coach Alumbaugh if we could run it on national television. He said, "Sure." We were watching the successful fake punt on film the day after the game when he looked at me and said: "I didn't realize we were only at the 30-yard-line!"

It's also important to make sure the kids know a trick play is coming and are not surprised. Not only do we work on them all week, but I tell them to "be ready because we might run this" again and again. I let them know the specific game situation we're looking for, so they don't freak out. Kids lose their minds during games sometimes. I always try to gather them on the sideline before any special teams play and let them know what we're doing so they're prepared.

CHAPTER 7

Offseason Conditioning

As long as we had that weight room, we could be champions.

—Former De La Salle head coach Bob Ladouceur

When I first took the job at De La Salle in 1979, I was so disappointed that we didn't have a weight room or weights because I knew that regardless of how much I taught the kids technique-wise that if they didn't have some foundation of strength behind it, they were not going to be successful.

In other words we couldn't win without weights.

I tore apart an old equipment room. One of the Christian Brothers, who was one of my earliest mentors, bought me an Olympic bar out of his own pocket because he knew how important it was to me. One of my first assistant coaches welded together three benches. I had all the kids bring in weights and bars they had at home and I pieced together a 20-circuit training station by using an adjacent shower room. We lifted outdoors. I put together an 80-minute workout, and they got gassed and they got stronger. Sometimes a coach has to use his ingenuity. Don't complain about what you don't have and do what you can do.

People thought our weight room was a joke, and it was, but as long as we had a weight room, I didn't care. If we had a stadium that only seated 300, I wouldn't have cared. If we didn't have balls or whistles, I wouldn't have cared. As long as we had that weight room, we could be champions. I understood how much lifting weights helped me as a player. But it had to be challenging, it had to have a rhyme and a reason. It needed to be monitored and coached. You can't just open the doors and say go lift. I was consistent, insistent, ready, prepared, and kept an attendance sheet on a big board I hung up on the wall so everybody could see who was making it and who wasn't.

I trained the kids myself for the first 15 years, and what helped me was that I was in great shape and always continued lifting with them. I was way stronger than every player I had. I was an example for those guys, too. I remember always telling them that the fact that I was stronger than any of them was not a good thing.

Finally, we built our new weight room in 1985. By then, we had won two section championships without a legitimate weight room. You don't need the latest and greatest—just dedicated kids and a place to lift and run.

Our offseason conditioning program has evolved over the years thanks to former trainer Mike Blasquez, who is now the director of strength and conditioning for University of California, Berkeley athletics, and Coach Alumbaugh, but I think we were pioneers in some ways, even

The only focus while lifting weights is on getting bigger, faster, and stronger in a safe way. We don't play music, allow for chitchat, or horse around. (Photo by Bob Larson)

back in the early days. We incorporated footwork, exploding from our stances, and using the proper steps. I don't remember anybody else pulling tires, and now they sell sleds that can be loaded with weights and pulled. Pulling tires was just something we thought of and figured out how to do ourselves. It was old school.

The Culture

Football is a very violent, physically challenging game that requires a year-round commitment to conditioning and weight lifting. You can't get guys in good enough shape to play football if your conditioning program starts in June. We've always gone year round. We're not just trying to get the kids in shape, but we're also trying to bring them together as a team and teach accountability. You don't teach accountability by giving them six months off.

Our No. 1 job is to keep them safe while they play a game that requires high-speed collisions, and they're not safe if they are running around and taking and making hits in anything less than the best physical condition possible. Besides, what would parents rather have them doing between 3:00 and 5:00 PM?

It takes a lot of time to get kids in that kind of shape, and much of it comes during the summer, when coaches are trying to take vacations and make up for lost time with the family. A lot of coaches have told us they don't want to spend as much time on conditioning as we do. We understand that. We just view it differently. Getting our kids in shape is a constant, tedious grind, but it's absolutely essential to what we do.

We don't get a lot of pushback from parents or players for three reasons, the first being we've had a track record of sustained success. Secondly, the kids need to see the results, and we deliver results. They can see themselves getting stronger and more defined. They can feel themselves getting faster, quicker, and more confident and aggressive. They know they're becoming better players.

The third reason is our offseason work ethic has become part of our culture, and it's the kids who created it and continue to honor it. That culture is based on a no-frills attitude. There is no music, no mirrors, and no horsing around in our weight room. You show up, you shut up, and you get to work. We don't keep them in there all day. We get them in. We get them working. We get them out. No one sits; everybody is watching and encouraging or spotting or changing weights. There's no rest, no chitchat. Nobody is talking about what they're going to do tonight or tomorrow. It's all strictly business. What are we in here for? Not to socialize, play around, or squeak by. We're here to get strong and work hard. That's the bottom line. Everything we do is geared toward that. Otherwise, people open that weight room, and they're in there for three hours. We want them done quickly. We want our workouts to be as close as we can get to game tempo.

Kids want to quit. They claim they're not having any fun. The fun comes when our work is done. The reward is on the backside. Do you want to be a good football player and play at the highest level? If so, they have to resign themselves to the fact that a large part of the conditioning program is not going to be fun.

You need to put in the time and endure the pain.

When you take that approach, guys band together and become a tight-knit group. I think that's a dynamic of all groups. If you give them a difficult task, they band together or fall apart. We do other things to create team, but the hard work galvanizes them into a tough unit. They become friends. You put anybody through the pressure cooker, and they're going to come together and form friendships that last a long time, that go beyond the field for sure. That's part of what we do here. Our guys are really, really tough kids because they have to be.

A lot of kids can't make the commitment. We started with 92 kids in January of 2014 and started fall practice with a roster in the 60s, which is normal for us. That's okay. That's the way it's supposed to be. Very rarely do we cut kids. If you can make it through the offseason conditioning program and prove you're committed and not an injury risk, you have earned a spot on our team. If you can get through the work we put you through, you've earned the jersey.

We work out for 90 minutes four days a week after school. We warm up, lift, work on our footwork, go through agility stations, condition, and then stretch. Our kids are still on their way home by 4:45 PM because we don't mess around. The workouts are intense. The kids are always moving even when they're in the weight room. That's part of the conditioning.

The weight room is also open before school. Kids participating in spring sports lift in the morning for one hour. They don't do conditioning or agility. They should be getting that while participating in their spring sport anyway. They just lift. The spring sport coaches at our school are on board with that. We get asked a lot about the support we receive from our spring coaches. We get support because we get results. Our baseball coach loves our football guys because those guys are ripping the ball. The best hitters on the team are usually the football players.

Coach Alumbaugh was the same way when we had him as a player. He was one of our strongest guys and he was a great baseball player. He came in in the mornings and did his morning workouts and then practiced baseball after school. He was big and strong and was ripping the cover off the ball, hitting .500. Then his senior year when he was done with football, he thought he would go the way of a lot of other seniors and quit lifting. He slumped during the first four games of the season. I saw him one day and noticed he had a little gut. I asked him, "Are you still lifting?" He said he hadn't been lifting. I said, "No wonder you're in a slump. Look at what you did last year and what you're doing now." He started lifting and pretty soon he was killing it again.

If a kid participating in spring sports misses the morning lifting session, he lifts with us in the afternoon before going out to the track or the baseball diamond. If there's a big game or a big track meet, you have to be reasonable about it, but they have to make four lifts a week. These guys are 16, 17, and 18. Even if they lift at seven in the morning, they will have recovered by the time the baseball game starts at 3:30. They will be okay. The spring sport coaches agree with us on that.

If you're not participating in a spring sport, you are expected to be at the afternoon workouts. Because the weight room is open in the morning and after school, student-athletes can make up a workout in the morning if they have to go to a driver's test or a doctor's appointment after school. People ask, "What's your attendance?" We tell them it's 100 percent. There's no such thing as a missed workout because if you can't come at night, you come in the morning and vice versa. No excuses. Everybody is equal. It's important that everybody puts in the same amount of work, everybody's accountable, and the training becomes engrained.

We'll have a kid come up and say he couldn't work out after school because, for example, he had to go to San Francisco to have dinner for his grandmother's birthday. He said he has to leave at 4:30 PM. We were like, "No, you're not going at 4:30. If that was prearranged, and you told us a few days ago, we could've figured out something else." A lot of coaches would let him go because it's his grandmother's birthday. We don't buy that. We said, "When is the reservation?" He said 7:30 PM. *And you want to leave by 4:30?* He said he had to go home and get his clothes. We said, "Why didn't you bring your clothes to school so you could change in the locker room after your workout and save time?" He said he hadn't thought about that. Then came the parade of lame excuses. We told him to call his mom and fix it. His mom ended up bringing his dress clothes to school, and he worked out just like everybody else, changed, and made it to his grandmother's birthday dinner with time to spare.

The older kids help the younger kids get through it. They teach them how we work. We might have a guy come up and say, "I can't make running today because I forgot my shoes." He might be next to another kid who is going to be a senior and he just shakes his head. The senior kid says, "Man, we don't do that around here. Guys have extra shoes. I don't care if you have to run barefoot, you're running." Everybody has to find a way to get work done and not make an excuse to miss work just like in real life. Kids often feel ashamed if they're banned from workouts because they're not working hard enough or not showing up. The whole idea is you can't get out of work, and that's an important life lesson.

If you do have to miss a workout, communicate with your coach and make up the lift. If there's a day off from school from January through May, we give the kids a day off from workouts. Otherwise, you're expected to be there. If guys are flaking out or not showing up or not working hard, they can't be part of the program because it undermines the accountability and teamwork.

We start our offseason conditioning program when school resumes after Christmas break in January. For varsity players that means their season will have ended two weeks before, but the JV kids have had two months of nothing, so we focus on core work and don't run them a bunch in the beginning. We're just trying to get them in the weight room and concentrating on body weight and movement. In February we start lowering our reps in what we call a conversion to power. We want them strong and able to convert that strength to powerful movements, which is why we do so many Olympic lifts.

When summer starts it's still four days a week, but we lengthen the time a little bit and do lower reps because we're really trying to build strength. Two days a week, on Mondays and Fridays, we do heavy, heavy conditioning.

Another huge focus of our offseason conditioning program is footwork. It's all about keeping their feet moving, getting their hips turned in space, and staying balanced. We have a lot of agility stations. We make them run through ropes. We do tight figure eights and shuttle runs to get them quicker. A De La Salle football team is quick. We are constantly working on footwork. I used to think we worked on it more than most teams, but that has changed in recent years. A lot of teams have picked that up, and it has become a major part of a lot of programs.

We run on the track. We run liners. We pull tires. Pulling tires builds toughness. We schedule our passing leagues on Tuesdays and Thursdays. That's when we lift and do position-specific drill work and condition-specific footwork drills. The linemen flip tractor tires, pull tires, and hit the sled. The running backs do snake work with the quarterback. We pull more tires. Receivers run deep routes at full speed. We'll play seven on seven.

We have 36 summer workouts. You need to be at 30 to be at top physical shape to be ready when the season starts. We offer a couple make-up opportunities if players had to miss workouts during the summer. We also give the kids the week of Fourth of July off and we give them another few days at the beginning of August. We make sure the parents are very aware of this schedule so vacations can be planned accordingly. We encourage them to take their vacations during these times. If you can't get your vacation in, well, we apologize, but you can't leave for two-and-a-half months in the summer and come back and play football for us.

We never use conditioning to punish kids. Every once in a while, if we're jumping offside and not concentrating during a practice, I might have them run a gasser to get their attention and to get them to focus. But we don't use it for punishment because it takes the focus off the conditioning itself, and conditioning is a critical part of our preparation. If you have two-way players, if you want to win the third and fourth quarters, you have to be in good shape. It's critical.

We ban our kids from working out if they are struggling in a class, smart off to a teacher, or require other discipline. That has been a very effective tool for us. They sit in the breezeway between our locker room and weight room, do their homework, and watch their teammates train, and it really bothers them. It becomes a major motivation for them to get their grades up or to start treating people with respect because they know their friends are getting faster and stronger, and they can only watch.

Our conditioning program is a big reason why I can't remember a kid transferring here in the summer and being able to play for us. If a kid comes in here as a junior, they are already so far behind the curve in terms of what we put our kids through that they get blown out of the water. They are the weakest kids in the weight room, the slowest on the track. Time and time again, a kid shows up who admissions lets in and he wants to play football. It's usually during the summer. This has happened at least five or six times during the past 10 years or so. They show up, get in our summer conditioning program for a week, and are back at their old schools because they can't keep up. That happens all the time.

Strength and Conditioning

By De La Salle strength training and conditioning coach Mark Wine

According to our mission statement, the focus of strength and conditioning at De La Salle High School is to enhance the athletes' sport and life performance through fundamentals, proper technique, Olympic movements, functional training, and hard work. Disciplined and dedicated coaches will integrate exercise science into the individual sports' strength and conditioning programs with the goal of developing every athlete in every sport to their maximum potential. We understand that the weight room allows our athletes to stay healthy while hitting hard and moving fast throughout a long and physical season.

In order for us to achieve this training, it starts the moment our athletes get to De La Salle. The first year our athletes are introduced to an intensive conditioning program. The focus is on general conditioning, lifting technique, and general strength. This first year is about teaching the young athletes about work ethic and dedication to each other. We then transition into focused strength and conditioning training programs that result in dedicated, powerful, strong, and healthy athletes. The athlete goes through vast changes physically and mentally as they mature into young men during their remaining years. Our conditioning must be on point 100 percent of the time, which is why we place so much emphasis on it. If an athlete chooses to continue his career at the collegiate level, our goal is to have him be a top performer in the weight room upon arrival.

Here are the key focuses of all of the athletes so that they develop through progression, digression, and strength and power:

- **Development of the athlete**—starts at the clinic and camp level and continues through freshman year.

- **Speed**—starts in and ends in the weight room. Speed is simply an application of force upon the ground. De La Salle athletes are put through properly coached lifts that focus on technique, load, and depth.

- **Strength**—through the mind, body, and soul. The boys are put through the ringer in the weight room through stringent discipline, heavy-loaded movements, and high levels of expectations to give 110 percent every time they step through the door.

- **Power**—to develop athletic prowess on the field, court, grid iron, diamond, track, pool, and course. Power lifting is a very difficult form of exercise that must be performed with caution and responsibility...hence the next bullet.

- **Progression and digression**—we have designed and currently implement such workouts like the Spartan Assessment and the First Spartan to effectively advance the athletes at DLS through levels of training. Not everyone is at the same level or phase in their training program. We understand the necessary steps it takes to squat properly, power clean properly, deadlift properly, and so on. Building the DLS athlete up is what makes DLS winners both on and off the field and both in and out of the weight room.

- **Olympic weightlifting**—is the style of lifting that is most important to an athlete's performance. However, this style of lifting must be performed 100 percent correctly to be effective; therefore, the athletes at DLS are advanced to this level.

- **Injury prevention**—starts in the weight room. Strength and conditioning at DLS understands the importance of dynamic movements, proprioceptive training, supplementary training, depth jumps, and eccentric focused training. Exercises that place emphasis on highly injured movement patterns can be an effective tool in reducing injury to athletes. For example, depth jumps are an effective tool at reducing the likelihood of injury during deceleration or impact of sprinting because they prepare the body for the specific muscular requirements and stresses that are placed on the knees and lower extremities.

DLS FOOTBALL CONDITIONING PROGRAM

Phase I—Pre-Conditioning
- **Primary Focus**—Olympic technique and mobility
- **Secondary Focus**—body preparation for resistance (i.e. bodyweight core-focused circuits)

Example Day
1. Warm Up I: dynamic and movement specific
2. Agility Ladder: hop scotch—icky—carioca—lat 1 in 1out
3. Mobility Drills: rainbows—overheads—winner rack
4. Olympic Technique
   a. lift off to position x 2
   b. clean high pull
   c. power cleans
5. BDWT Preparation: BDWT LB/TB
   a. squat jumps (on cue) x 8 E
   b. push up arm extensions x 8 P
   c. sprinter lunges x 12 E P
   d. push up plank transition x 8 E
   e. split leg windmill x 12 S E
   f. V-sit twists (w/ 10 lb plate or MB) x 30 F
   g. burpee jumps x 8 E F
6. Partner Stretch: OH push—Russian—cross over—PNF hams—hip c/r

Phase II—Offseason I
- **Primary Focus**—hypertrophy and strength development
- **Olympic Focus**—master the pull for cleans and snatch pulls
- **Conditioning**—general
- **Injury Focus**—eliminate major asymmetry

Example UB Lift—Lift 4 of the week
1. hang power snatch x 5 (65-75 percent)
Wingspan 3 x 6
2. military press/ 12, 10, 8, 8, 8 (# reps)
>>bent over rows/ 12, 10, 8, 8, 8 (# reps)
3. incline dumbbell bench/ 12, 10, 8, 8 (# reps)
>>pull-up complex (bigs: pulldown complex) x 4 E
4. squat to press/ 3 x 8
>>HR: burpee slam/ 3 x 15

Phase III—Offseason II
- **Primary Focus**—strength and hypertrophy
- **Olympic Focus**—cleans w/ full squat catches, hang power snatch/pulls
- **Conditioning**—general, speed, and agility
- **Injury Focus**—eliminate major asymmetry

Phase IV—Preseason
- **Primary Focus**—power and explosive strength
- **Olympic Focus**—max power and complexes
- **Conditioning**—sprint ability, sport-specific agility/footwork
- **Injury Focus**—mobility, hip stability, and shoulders

Example HIIT Circuit Bar Complexes—S&C coach sets the weight standards
SPARTAN UP (groups of 2 only) x 4—track time
1. hang power clean x 4
2. power jerk x 6
3. front squat x 8
4. bent over row x 10
5. push ups x 12
    → run 400 yards (4 laps)

Phase V—In-Season
- **Primary Focus**—power and strength maintenance
- **Olympic Focus**—bar complexes
- **Conditioning**—sprint ability and sport-specific drills
- **Injury Focus**—mobility and on the fly

Example of a Post-Gameday Lift—Recovery Eccentric Focus
1. tempo squats 3-4 x 6
2. one arm bench 4 x 8 E
>>Aztec rows 4 x 8 E
3. overhead split squats 3 x 12 E
4. IYTI 2-3 x 8 S
>>adduction 2-3 x 12 E
>>donkeys 2-3 x 12 S E
6. Turkish get ups 2 x 3 E

E= Explosive
P= With a pause
S= Slow
F= Fast

||||||||||||||||||||||||||||||||||||||||||||||||||||||||||||||||||||||||||||||||||||||||||||||||

Spring Football
By current De La Salle head coach Justin Alumbaugh

The idea behind spring football is somewhat outdated in California. It used to be the only time teams could use actual footballs except for passing-league tournaments, but now we're allowed to do everything we do during the spring at our summer workouts, which start two weeks after spring practice ends.

Since we're not allowed to be in pads, though, spring football turns into extended conditioning and weight training sessions where we introduce players to the speed and tempo of practice and what we're going to want them to do once we get in pads. We start with the very basics and assume nothing. We talk about splits, stance, our numbering system, and other fundamental concepts.

Because a lot of our best players are playing baseball or lacrosse or competing in track, we get to spend quality time with the junior varsity kids so we can get an idea for where they are in their development, whether they can help us, and what they need to work on during the summer.

The linemen begin an up-close and personal relationship with the blocking sled. Our linemen do their agility drills and drill work, flip tires, hit the sled, and lift weights. We will unroll the snake, and the running backs, receivers, and defensive backs are out there longer doing ballhandling drills and running routes and learning to run those routes at the proper depth. It's the start of what's to come and the first time this group is together as a team. It gives the coaching staff a glimpse of individual personalities and the team dynamic. We learn how they interact, how much respect they have for each other, and how well they work together.

At the end of the week, we come together and run some plays and do some teamwork just to get them excited about being out there. Mostly, it's a gateway to our summer workouts. After spring ball ends, we give them a week off and then start our four-day-a-week summer program. Here's a typical spring schedule:

Spring Football Schedule
Monday
3:00–4:00—Lift
4:00–4:15–Agility stations
4:15–4:45—Individual offense
4:45–5:15—7 on 7, linemen hit defensive sled
5:15—Conditioning

Tuesday

3:00–4:00—Lift

4:00–4:15—Liners

4:15–4:45—Individual defense

4:45–5:15—7 on 7, lineman offensive sled

Wednesday

3:15–3:45—Agility stations

3:45–4:15—Individual offense

4:15–4:45—7 on 7, linemen defensive sled

4:45–5:15—Teamwork

5:15–5:30—Pull tires

Thursday

3:00–4:00—Lift

4:00–4:15—Agility stations

4:15–4:45—Individual offense

4:45–5:15—7 on 7, linemen hit defensive sled

5:15—Conditioning

Friday

3:00–4:00—Lift

4:00–4:15—Liners

4:15–4:45—Individual defense

4:45–5:15—7 on 7, linemen offensive sled

|||||||||||||||||||||||||||||||||||||||||||||||||||||||||||||||||||||||||||||||||||||||||||||||||||

Passing Leagues

By former De La Salle head coach Bob Ladouceur

We were in the finals of a passing league tournament a couple years ago, and the opposing team ran every play out of a shotgun formation, which isn't what they do during the regular season. The quarterback took the snap, pump faked left, looked right, and looked left again. They were putting four receivers in the pattern and sending their running back up the middle to split our zone, and I'm thinking, *What are they accomplishing?*

We take a much more practical approach. Passing league is a great time to run your defense against certain sets that you will see during the season. Obviously, defenses always face a tough challenge during passing leagues because there's no pass rush, but it's a good time to work on situations like third and long and goal line. We work our nickel package a lot. Everything we work on is actually what we run during the season. If we get ripped in passing league, we're not going to adjust our defense. We run what we run, and it gives the kids a chance to get used to our concepts.

Passing league really gives our defensive backs a lot of work. They spend most of their time playing against our offense in practice, and we're not a throwing team. Several of our traditional opponents aren't either. Then all of a sudden, an opponent will come along with wideouts all over the field. Passing league offers a great opportunity to prepare us for an unusual opponent like that. For example, we never had faced the kind of wide-open offense we knew we would see when we played St. Louis (of Honolulu, Hawaii) High during the 2002 season. We worked against that offense during the summer and in passing league and we were ready.

Passing league also gives us an opportunity to play different combinations of guys and see what they can do against real competition. It helps us put our depth chart together heading into fall practice. For those guys who think they should be playing and aren't on the depth chart, it's an opportunity to show us what they can do. That's where they can earn playing time. When I was the head coach, we never ran play-action passes during passing league. I didn't see the point. It's hard to get a good look because the opposing defense knows it's going to be a pass, and they bail out of there.

What I did was incorporate play-action passes into team work so the quarterback and receivers got a better look and then cut down the time we worked on seven-on-sevens in practice and replaced it with more team work.

Coach Alumbaugh runs play-action passes during passing league, and we still get guys open. Coach Panella might tell the quarterback, "Don't worry, the linebacker isn't going to be there in a game, but it's the right spot." We try to keep it as realistic as possible. We, for example, don't want them taking a three-step drop but somehow releasing the ball at the line of scrimmage. If it's a 14-yard curl route, we don't want the receiver to run it at eight yards just to make a first down in passing league. We don't run any exotic offenses during passing leagues like a lot of people do. They might put five wide receivers out there. If they did that against us in a game, we would sack them every time. A lot of our routes are two and three-receiver routes because we keep our backs in to block just like we would during the season.

CHAPTER 8

Sports Medicine

If kids leave feeling broke and beaten and move away from sports because they had a bad experience, we have failed.

—De La Salle head athletic trainer Kent Mercer

There can be a lot of pressure to get kids on the field as soon as possible or back in time for a big game, but none of that matters if the athlete isn't ready. We will not put an athlete on the field if it might jeopardize his health or potentially causes him more harm regardless of the circumstances. Our coaches understand that and wholeheartedly support it.

It's all about a shared vision and communication between administrators, coaches, parents, athletes, our team physician, and the training staff so everyone understands that we want student-athletes to compete as soon as it's safe to do so.

Athletes compete in high school sports for a very short period of time. We want them to leave with a better understanding of themselves, their bodies, and how to prepare for recreational sports and activities later in life. If kids leave feeling broke and beaten and move away from sports because they had a bad experience, we have failed. We're always looking to improve and refine our sports medicine program to benefit the student-athlete and increase performance.

Team Physician

By De La Salle head athletic trainer Kent Mercer and De La Salle team physician Dr. Charles Preston

It is our opinion that every high school athletic department should make an effort to find a team physician because it's a mutually beneficial relationship that can help a physician's practice grow tremendously while reassuring administrators, coaches, parents, and student-athletes that medical decisions are being handled appropriately.

The school administration, sports medicine staff, and the prospective physician should make their expectations clear from the beginning. Our football program's expectations for our team physician is that they attend all home and away football games. They are to use any and all resources at their disposal, including for injuries that fall outside their area of expertise, to the benefit of the student-athlete. They must see student-athletes at their office as soon as possible regardless of insurance details and/or expedite the care of student-athletes who use physicians from other health-care providers to ensure they are seen promptly.

The physician's expectation is that the coaching staff, administration, and sports medicine staff never second-guess or question the physician's decisions. It's important to show a united front when a parent, for example, wants their child back on the field before the team physician deems it safe.

Administrators, the coaching staff, the sports medicine staff, and the team physician must know their jobs and do their jobs amidst an atmosphere of mutual trust and respect where everyone supports one another in doing what's best not for the team or the school but for each individual athlete.

Sports Medicine Mission Statement

In support of the school's primary goals of spiritual, intellectual, and physical development of its students, the mission of the sports medicine department is to support the athlete as a whole spiritually, mentally, and physically. The health and welfare of the student athlete shall be paramount in the department.

De La Salle strives to develop a program that effectively utilizes the talents of the staff and resources of the program. A diversified program of prevention, evaluation, education, treatment, and rehabilitation will assure a positive healthy recovery experience, an improved quality of life, a safe return to full athletic participation, and continued athletic success. In addition to injury management, student-athlete education will be emphasized to instill lifelong healthy practices.

‖‖‖

Concussions

By De La Salle head athletic trainer Kent Mercer and De La Salle assistant athletic trainer Doug Bauman

DE LA SALLE HIGH SCHOOL

Concussion Information Sheet

A concussion is a brain injury, and all brain injuries are serious. They are caused by a bump, blow, or jolt to the head or by a blow to another part of the body with the force transmitted to the head. They can range from mild to severe and can disrupt the way the brain normally works. Even though most concussions are mild, all concussions, are potentially serious and may result in complications, including prolonged brain damage and death if not recognized and managed properly. In other words even a ding or a bump on the head can be serious. You can't see a concussion, and most sports concussions occur without loss of consciousness. Signs and symptoms of concussion may show up right after the injury or can take hours or days to fully appear.

Symptoms may include one or more of the following:

- Headaches
- Pressure in head
- Nausea or vomiting
- Neck pain
- Balance problems or dizziness
- Blurred, double, or fuzzy vision
- Sensitivity to light or noise

- Feeling sluggish or slowed down
- Feeling foggy or groggy
- Drowsiness
- Change in sleep patterns
- Amnesia
- Not feeling right
- Fatigue or low energy
- Sadness
- Nervousness or anxiety
- Irritability
- More emotional
- Confusion
- Concentration or memory problems (forgetting game plays)
- Repeating the same question/comment

Signs observed by teammates, parents, and coaches include:

- Appears dazed
- Vacant facial expression
- Confused about assignment
- Forgets plays
- Is unsure of game, score, or opponent
- Moves clumsily or displays incoordination
- Answers questions slowly
- Slurred speech
- Shows behavior or personality changes
- Can't recall events prior to hit
- Can't recall events after hit
- Seizures or convulsions
- Any change in typical behavior or personality
- Loses consciousness

What can happen if my child keeps on playing with a concussion or returns too soon?

Athletes with the signs and symptoms of concussion should be removed from play immediately. Continuing to play with the signs and symptoms of a concussion leaves the young athlete especially vulnerable to greater injury. There is an increased risk of significant damage from a concussion for a period of time after that concussion occurs, particularly if the athlete suffers another concussion before completely recovering from the first one. This can lead to prolonged recovery or even to severe brain swelling (second impact syndrome) with devastating and even fatal consequences. It is well known that adolescent or teenage athletes will often under report symptoms of injuries, and concussions are no different. As a result, education of administrators, coaches, parents, and students is the key for student-athletes' safety.

If you think your child has suffered a concussion

Any athlete even suspected of suffering a concussion should be removed from the game or practice immediately. No athlete may return to activity after an apparent head injury or concussion, regardless of how mild it seems or how quickly symptoms clear without medical clearance. Close observation of the athlete should continue for several hours. The new CIF Bylaw 313 now requires implementation of long and well-established return-to-play concussion guidelines that have been recommended for several years: "A student-athlete who is suspected of sustaining a concussion or head injury in a practice or game shall be removed from competition at that time and for the remainder of the day."

"A student-athlete who has been removed may not return to play until the athlete is evaluated by a licensed heath care provider trained in the evaluation and management of concussion and received written clearance to return to play from that health care provider."

You should also inform your child's coach if you think that your child may have a concussion. Remember it's better to miss one game than miss the whole season. And when in doubt, the athlete sits out.

Student-athlete Name Printed	Student-athlete Signature	Date

Parent/Legal Guardian Name Printed	Parent/Legal Guardian Signature	Date

Concussion Awareness
By defensive and special teams coordinator Terry Eidson

A full-time athletic trainer should be at every practice and game to ensure evaluations are made by medical professionals and not a coach who has a championship game on his mind and only a few hours of concussion-related training. It's in everyone's best interest to have an athletic trainer who can make a diagnosis as incidents occur and take the decision-making power out of the coach's hands.

Education is key. We want parents and players to be educated because it gives us more eyes and ears watching and listening to what players are doing and saying. Coaches can get caught up in a game or practice and might not recognize when a player has gotten dinged. On many occasions during games, it has been the kids who tell us if someone has a problem. They can often see and hear things we can't so we make sure they are educated and looking for potential signs. They might notice that a teammate doesn't know where he is or what down it is, inform us, and we immediately remove the player from the game. We once had a player call a timeout during a playoff game because he was concerned about his teammate. It was absolutely the right thing to do. Whenever I see a kid stagger, I immediately take him out of the game for evaluation.

Every year our players undergo a cognitive test that we use as a baseline if a player is suspected of having a concussion, and we have a neuropsychologist and a neurologist that we work with to help determine when it's appropriate for an athlete to begin a progression back to activity.

If a player has any type of significant head injury, even if it's just seeing stars, he's out for a week. Any type of concussion, regardless of whether it involves memory loss or not knowing where they are, requires a minimum of two weeks. There's no debate. We understand and agree with this as coaches. We take it extremely seriously and we honor the necessary recovery time.

If a player gets two concussions in a season, he's done, and we have to discuss whether he can play the following year. We had a kid come back after having two concussions in one season only to have another five weeks later. We told him his football career at De La Salle was done. We don't mess with it.

» NUTRITION AND HYDRATION

Proper nutrition and hydration will allow the student-athlete to perform optimally. Food and drink act as the athlete's fuel, and without sound nutrition and hydration, an athlete will not be able to perform at his highest level. The two following examples (where the athlete is the car and food/drinks are the gasoline) help simplify the importance of nutrition and hydration:

- Imagine trying to drive a car without any gasoline; it will not run.
- Now, imagine driving a high-end sports car but fueling it with low-quality gasoline; it is not going to function at its highest potential.

The athlete needs to be very conscious about what he is putting in his body—what fuel he is using. Failure to do so will likely result in some type of decrease in performance.

Daily Guidelines

It is important to point out that a high school-aged male should consume approximately 2,500 to 4,000 calories per day, and these caloric needs increase with activity. For females this number is around 2,200 calories per day. Nutrition labels on foods and beverages are based on a 2,000-calorie diet so these need to be adjusted for high school-aged males and females.

When figuring out how much "fuel" one should consume, the following numbers should guide you:

- Carbohydrates should make up 55 to 60 percent of an individual's daily caloric intake.
- Fats should make up 25 to 30 percent of an individual's daily caloric intake (with most of this coming from unsaturated and polyunsaturated fats).
- Protein should make up 12 to 15 percent of an individual's daily caloric intake. (Note: most athletes already consume two to three times the daily recommended amount.)
- With regard to hydration, an individual should drink eight to 10 cups (64 to 80 fluid ounces) of water per day.

General Nutrition Tips

Eating frequently throughout the day can help to keep your energy up for workouts and classes. In order to achieve this benefit, keep your body moving on an energy surplus during the day and follow these tips:

- Always begin your day with breakfast even if it is something small.
- Eat a meal every three to four hours.
- Don't be afraid to snack during the day or after your evening meal. If you are hungry, you need to be fed but make good choices.
- Understand your body and hunger cues rather than watching a clock to determine when to eat.
- Your activity level will dictate how many calories you consume in a day. If your activity level is down, don't continue to eat as if you were practicing every day.
- Plan ahead for your day as it will allow you to have meals and snacks at appropriate times.
- Try to eat a high-energy snack prior to workouts such as a cereal bar, grapes, apple juice, or sports drink.
- Consume carbohydrates and proteins within two hours following a workout.
- Vary your diet and sources of protein.
- Try to consume eight to 10 servings of fruits and vegetables per day, working up to 12 to 13 servings per day.
- Check the color of your urine to help determine hydration status. Dark-colored urine can be a sign of a dehydrated state. Light-colored urine (the color of lemonade) indicates that you are appropriately hydrated.
- To make a successful change in weight (either up or down), it should be done over time. Do not try to gain or lose weight quickly because you will usually compromise your energy level or overall performance.
- Log your exercise and eating daily to better understand and reach your goal.

» PRE-ACTIVITY NUTRITION/HYDRATION

A pregame meal should be consumed three to six hours prior to the event. This meal should be balanced but should avoid large amounts of fat and protein as these nutrients are harder to digest. It is important that the athlete consume foods that he has eaten before to avoid gastrointestinal issues.

To allow for adequate digestion, the athlete should eat a pregame snack that is rich in carbohydrates but is not too heavy. Carbohydrates are the primary source of energy; thus it is important to have an ample amount of them prior to the event. For some athletes it may be difficult to eat this close to the activity because of pregame anxiety, but even a small amount of carbohydrates has been shown to help improve performance. Fifteen minutes prior to a training session, a small snack can be consumed. Again this snack should be light and consist of carbohydrates. (Examples include fruit juice, crackers, and pretzels.)

Hydration

During activity it is recommended that the athlete hydrate to replace fluids lost through sweat. This is very important as it helps one function optimally by regulating body processes, maintaining cellular balance, and preventing heat illness. It is recommended that athletes drink approximately eight ounces of water every 20 minutes of activity, and these needs increase if you are a heavy sweater. Replacing lost water is vital in optimizing athletic performance. Our bodies do not tell us we are thirsty until we have lost 1.5 to 2 percent of our body weight. Therefore, if an individual waits until he is thirsty to drink, then he is already at a disadvantage. Research has shown that as little as 1.5 to 2 percent dehydration can result in decreased performance; thus, it is important to be proactive and avoid this to function at one's highest potential.

Before talking about the positive effects of sports drinks, it is prudent to identify what classifies as a sports drink. Sports drinks are not the same as energy drinks. Sports drinks, like Gatorade, are electrolyte-enhanced

beverages that usually contain carbohydrates as well. Sports drinks
are highly beneficial to athletic performance and should be consumed
during prolonged or intense performance. As mentioned earlier athletes
sweat when they train, but the sweat is not just water. Instead, sweat is
a mixture of water and electrolytes (sodium, potassium, calcium, etc.).
The white lines that can be seen on baseball hats and undershirts worn
during activity are salt (sodium) stains that stay there after the water has
evaporated.

Sports drinks help replenish the electrolytes lost in sweat, and they also
provide carbohydrates that help replenish one's primary energy supply.
Failure to replenish both of these nutrients can lead to decreased energy,
electrolyte imbalances, and muscle cramping (which happens as a result
of electrolyte loss), all of which will result in decreased performance.

» POST-ACTIVITY CONSIDERATIONS

A postgame meal should be consumed within one to two hours of the
event. This meal should be well-balanced with carbohydrates, fats, and
proteins to replenish all of these nutrients that have been used during
participation. The athlete should also drink two to three cups of water
for every pound of body weight lost.

Within 30 minutes of a training session (and no more than two hours
after), the athlete should eat a post-training snack that consists of both
carbohydrates and a small amount of protein. The athlete should also
drink two to three cups of water for every pound of body weight lost.

Research has shown that carbohydrates consumed at 30 minutes
following training (and within a two-hour window after) results
in increased carbohydrates stores for the next training session.
Additionally, eating carbohydrates improves the body's ability to use
the protein to help repair muscle damage that occurred during training.
Protein consumption without carbohydrates is less effective at repairing
and building muscles tissue (aka protein synthesis). The athlete

should consume 1.0 to 1.5 grams of protein for every 2.2 pounds of body weight. (For example, a 180-pound athlete should consume approximately 81 to 122 grams of carbohydrates.)

Lastly, only a small amount of protein, 20 to 25 grams, needs to be ingested to stimulate protein synthesis. This is the equivalent of three ounces of chicken, beef, pork, or fish. If this is done repeatedly (five to six times throughout the day), muscle protein synthesis will be maximized. Protein amounts over 20 to 25 grams have not been shown to produce any increase in muscle protein synthesis. In fact, repeated overingestion of protein can actually have a negative effect on the body's ability to make muscle protein.

Here are examples of healthy recovery foods (courtesy of Dr. Jacqueline Berning, PhD, RD, CSSD)

- Energy or sports bars—19 to 50g carbohydrates, 10g protein
- Bagels with peanut or almond butter—58g carbohydrates, 16g protein
- Sub sandwiches—36g carbohydrates, 13g protein
- Granola with milk or yogurt—45g carbohydrates, 12g protein
- Crackers, cheese, and grapes—40g carbohydrates, 10g protein
- Vegetarian burritos with rice and beans—19g carbohydrates, 8g protein
- Fresh fruit like apples, bananas, oranges, grapes with low fat cheese—12 to 26g carbohydrates, 10g protein
- Vegetables such as carrots and celery with hummus and pita bread—25g carbohydrates, 10g protein
- Fruit smoothies (prepackaged)—16 ounces, 67g carbohydrates, 3g protein
- Smoothie with yogurt and milk—16 ounces, 50g carbohydrates, 10g protein
- Fruited yogurt and banana—one cup, 57g carbohydrates, 8g protein
- Trail mix—16g carbohydrates, 5g protein
- Chocolate milk—26g carbohydrates, 8g protein

- Animal crackers with almonds and banana—40g carbohydrates, 8g protein
- Sports drink—15g carbohydrates per 8 oz
- Recovery beverage—up to 40g carbohydrates, 10 to 20g protein

» SUPPLEMENTS

The athletic training staff at De La Salle encourages student-athletes to engage in sound nutrition practices and avoid supplements if possible. By practicing sound nutrition and eating healthy, one will not need to use supplements as he will already be ingesting all the needed nutrients for his goals. Additionally, eating nutritious foods has been proven to be more effective at delivering nutrients to the body.

Student-athletes need to understand that taking supplements has the potential to be dangerous. Supplements are not regulated by the Food and Drug Administration in the same way that foods are regulated; therefore they may contain dangerous ingredients. Supplements are also often produced in factories where other supplements may be produced, which can increase the risk of cross-contamination, and this means they may be ingesting a substance that is not on the ingredient list or is potentially a banned or unhealthy substance.

We encourage those individuals who are taking supplements to come and talk with us so that we can help them determine its relative safety and understand their rationale for taking the supplement. By speaking with us, we may be able to provide them with some healthier and more nutritious alternatives to meet their goals.

Acknowledgments

Every head coach knows that very little can be accomplished unless they have a staff of capable, dedicated coaches working beside them. I have been blessed throughout the years by having the best educators and teachers a head coach could hope for. The smartest thing I have ever done is hire great assistants and then get out of their way and let them coach their players. They have been and continue to be exceptional coaches.

Beloved by students and peers, Terry Eidson is the most talented teacher and coach I have ever known. I thank God he has been a critical part of my life the past 33 years. Terry and I have been compared to Oscar Madison and Felix Unger from *The Odd Couple*, and I admit we are odd. I don't think we could be more opposite personality-wise. However, we agree on everything when it comes to the philosophy and method of education and coaching. More importantly, I couldn't ask for a better friend.

I want to thank my family: Lissa, Suzy, Cathy, Tom, Liz, Pat, Greg, Jake, Olivia, and Brooke, and my children: Jennifer, Danny, Michael, and Sophia for always being there for me. Your love and support and having you on the sideline motivated me to make you proud of the job I did. I love you guys, and without you, my work would have been less meaningful.

To principal Brother Robert Wickman, president Mark DeMarco, and athletic directors Leo Lopoz and Derricke Brown, thank you for your support and for trusting me to run the football program. You made my job so much easier and enjoyable.

I'd like to thank three of the most competitive and most dynamic leaders I have ever had the privilege to coach: Patrick Walsh, Matt

Gutierrez, and Maurice Jones-Drew, as well as everyone else whom I have coached through the years.

A special thank you to Frank Allocco, a Hall of Fame coach in his own right, for believing in me and for our lengthy talks on coaching and motivation. I'd like to thank two outstanding mentors in my life. The first is Tony La Russa. I met Tony in the second half of my career, when he agreed to speak at our awards banquet. At that time we became friends and have often had a free exchange about coaching and managing. To have a coach who is mentioned in the same breath as Connie Mack and John McGraw to listen to and to learn from is truly amazing. This man is a genuine part of American history. Aside from his expertise in sports, I also discovered Tony is a modern Renaissance man—from sports to music, dance, leadership, and his Animal Rescue Foundation, Tony leaves no stone unturned. He's made me a better coach. I thank him for his interest in what I do and for his friendship.

Last, but certainly not least, I want to thank Mr. Ken Hofmann. Ken has been a father figure and mentor to me for 28 years. Part of the definition of mentor for me is "somebody you don't want to let down." Ken sponsored an awards banquet for our team in 1987 and got to know some of our players and coaches. From that point on, he has always been actively supportive of me and our teams. He believed in our methodology and the job I was doing. I never wanted to let him down and I took his support very seriously. In turn, Ken has supported the school in capital improvements, allowing our school to expand enrollment. Our new student activity center is named after him, and recently he is leading, along with his daughter, Lisa, the planning and execution of a new science and technology wing to our school. Ken is all about youth and education. His community youth center in Concord, California, services hundreds of kids in sports and educational services. Every city in America should have a youth center like his. He is a true visionary—tough and demanding, yet kind, fair, and generous. I admire him and thank him for his support.

About the Authors

Bob Ladouceur established himself as one of the most successful high school coaches in the country during his 33 years at De La Salle High School. He garnered the most victories in California history, 29 North Coast Section Championships, 19 California State Championships, five national championships, and 20 top 20 national finishes in his last 21 seasons. Despite stepping down as head coach after the 2013 season, Ladouceur continues to teach physical education and religious studies at De La Salle and serves as an assistant coach under his successor, former De La Salle player and longtime assistant coach Justin Alumbaugh. Ladouceur's website is coachlad.com.

Neil Hayes is the author of the best-selling and critically acclaimed book *When the Game Stands Tall: The Story of the De La Salle Spartans and Football's Longest Winning Streak* and the co-author of *The Last Putt: Two Teams, One Dream, and a Freshman Named Tiger*. He has been a sportswriter in Arizona, the San Francisco area, and with the *Chicago Sun-Times*. Hayes lives in the Chicago area with his wife, Charlee, and two children, Nick and Riley. His website is neilhayeswriter.com.